Battlegrour

CASSINO

Battleground Europe

CASSINO

Ian Blackwell

Pen & Sword
MILITARY

First published in Great Britain in 2005 by
Pen & Sword Military
an imprint of
Pen & Sword Books Ltd
47 Church Street
Barnsley
South Yorkshire
S70 2AS

ISBN 1 84415 235 9

A CIP catalogue record for this book is
available from the British Library

Typeset in Palatino

Printed and bound in the United Kingdom by CPI

Pen & Sword Books Ltd incorporates the Imprints of Pen & Sword Aviation,Pen
& Sword Maritime, Pen & Sword Military, Wharncliffe Local History, Pen and
Sword Select, Pen and Sword Military Classics and Leo Cooper.
For a complete list of Pen & Sword titles, please contact
Pen & Sword Books Limited
47 Church Street, Barnsley, South Yorkshire, S70 2AS, England
E-mail: enquiries@pen-and-sword.co.uk
Website: www.pen-and-sword.co.uk

CONTENTS

British troops crossing the Volturno in October 1943.

INTRODUCTION

At 0950 hours on 18 May 1944 soldiers from 12 Podolski Lancers raised a home-made regimental banner over the ruins of Monte Cassino Monastery. A bugler played the Hejnal, the medieval call which breaks off suddenly, commemorating the trumpeter whose call to the people of Kracow to take up arms was brought to an end when a Tartar arrow struck him in the throat. After five months of fighting, in which thousands of soldiers from at least eighteen nationalities bled and died,

Polish soldiers on Monte Cassino Monastery, 18 May 1944.
Polish Institute

the dominating symbol of the Gustav Line had fallen and the road to Rome up the Liri Valley was open.

To gain as full an understanding as possible of any battle it is necessary to visit the site and to consider the effects the ground had on its progress and outcome. Reading numerous accounts of any conflict from the comfort of one's armchair can aid the comprehension of issues such as the leadership shown by individuals or the advantages of one sort of weapon over another, but without placing everything in the context of the terrain over which the battle was fought the picture must remain incomplete. In most battles the ground plays a critical part, a factor well recognised by soldiers who consider it early on in their planning, but often largely ignored or misunderstood by those who try to interpret events from afar, usually with the help of maps which fail to highlight the contour lines sufficiently dramatically. Cassino is one battle in which the lie of the land dictated proceedings in a manner that was sometimes not fully appreciated by distant observers, such as Churchill, who became frustrated by the lack of progress and who cabled General Alexander to demand an explanation – which must have proved equally frustrating to Alexander who now had to turn his

Winston Churchill and General Sir Harold Alexander during the Prime Minister's visit to Italy in 1944.

attention from what he probably considered more important matters, such as fighting a war, to answer the Prime Minister's questions:

> '*I wish you would explain to me why this passage by Cassino Monastery Hill etc on a front of two or three miles is the only place which you must keep butting at. About five or six divisions have been worn out going into these jaws. Of course I do not know the ground or the battle conditions, but, looking at it from afar, it is puzzling why, if the enemy can be held and dominated at this point, no attacks can be made on the flanks. It seems very hard to understand why this most strongly defended point is the only way forward, or why, when it is saturated (in a military sense), ground cannot be gained on one side or the other...*'

Churchill to Alexander, 20 March 1944.

Alexander – or his staff – had to put together a reply and dispatch it the same day. The advances in technology which

'Fifth Army Fights General Weather' ran the headline caption accompanying this news release picture. It went on to say: 'Rain, wind, snow and frost have quickly followed one after the other, creating difficulty on the supply routes to the American Fifth Army front. Perseverance by all units to keep the roads open have resulted in constant supplies continuing to front line men fighting their battles for Cassino – the gateway to Rome.' The soldier is identified as Driver C. A. Langford, RASC of Boston, Lincs who, we are told, looks over the snow-covered peaks of the American-held sector on the Fifth Army front.

allowed this exchange to take place within the space of twenty-four hours were not always welcome.

The purpose of this book is to set the battle in the context of the ground and to assist the visitor to the site of the battle, not to try to emulate or outdo any of the excellent histories which have been written from the stance of grand strategy or political imperatives. While it takes the perspective of the terrain as a leading factor and attempts to explain the battles from a series of physical viewpoints, it cannot do justice to the wider picture. A volume this size can only give a broad overview of the campaign, with highlighted vignettes to help bring the history to life, and cannot give an entirely complete account. The serious reader is advised to dip into other works, the most comprehensive of which – to me – is John Ellis' *Cassino – the Hollow Victory*. Other titles include Matthew Parker's *Monte Cassino*, and the older *Cassino – Portrait of a Battle* by Fred Majdalany. From the German perspective, General von Senger und Etterlin's *Neither Fear nor Hope* has an interesting chapter on Cassino. Each of them has a different emphasis, and together they build up a comprehensive picture. There are also, of course, numerous formation and unit histories dealing with the subject, many of which I have consulted in the preparation for this work.

While many battlefields have been rendered almost unrecognisable by more recent development (motorways and housing programmes seem to pay little regard to the interests of the military historian), that of Cassino remains largely unspoilt. The mountains which form such an imposing backdrop have proved to be too large a challenge for the builders, and although there is far more vegetation on the battlefields now than in 1944 a good impression of the lie of the land can be gained. The principal differences between the war years and now are the towns, including Cassino and Sant' Angelo in Theodice, which had to be completely rebuilt after their destruction, although some of the road layout and sites such as the railway station are on their original locations; and the Castle, which has also been restored. The dual carriageway of the A1 Autostrada affects only part of the battlefield. The Monastery itself (see below) has been extensively restored to its former glory, but without the grime of centuries that had accumulated on its predecessor.

It gives me genuine pleasure to thank several individuals and organizations for their advice and assistance in writing this book, and for their permission to reproduce photographs and personal material. While researching it, I have had unstinting support from many people, and formed some new friendships. In particular, I have to thank Alessandro Campagna and Roberto Molle of the Associazone Battaglia di Cassino, "http://www.dalvolturnoacassino.it" and Federico Lamberti of Cassino, for having the patience to guide me around the battlefields and to answer my endless questions. Alessandro and Roberto also gave me permission to make use of photographs from their collection. Others who have been most generous with their photographs have been the Polish Institute and Sikorski Museum in London, the Gurkha Museum, and the New Zealand Electronic Text Centre ("http://www.nzetc.org").

Veterans of events sixty years ago are, unhappily, becoming thinner on the ground with each passing year. Two who seem not to have allowed the years to diminish their energy and enthusiasm are Michael Gibson-Horrocks, late of 2nd Battalion, the Royal Fusiliers, and Rudolf Valentin, late of the *1st Battalion Parachute Engineers*, both of whom have shared their memories with me to help my understanding of life in Italy in those violent months of 1944 – my grateful thanks goes to them for their time and kindness in reliving what cannot have been the most pleasant times of their lives. That they have been willing to do so is a reflection of their desire that the events of sixty years ago should not be forgotten, nor the lessons lost.

Practicalities

Timing of visits

As the battles for Cassino stretched from January to May, it could be argued that an appropriate date within those months would give a good feel for the particular phase of the conflict. However, the winter months are less likely to permit clear days, when maximum visibility over the valleys can be gained from the mountains; nor – as the reader will find from the text of this book – are good conditions to be relied upon then. However, should the intention be to relive as much as possible of the conditions of the time the visitor can chance his or her arm, and hope that the weather lives up to expectations!

The summer months can be extremely hot, and protection against sunburn and dehydration is advised. A further problem may be the heat haze, which can obscure the view to some extent. Whenever the visit is made, the journey is worth making.

Maps

Large-scale, up-to-date maps of the Cassino area are a distinct rarity, if they exist at all. The most informative ones are on a scale of 1:100,000, but these are based on originals surveyed in the 1940's and partially updated in the 1960's. They are almost impossible to obtain commercially, and the details on them relate neither to today nor to 1944. Nor are they of great value as a navigation aid – the autostrada is not shown, for example. The Touring Club Italiano Lazio 1:200,000 sheet is of some use in finding the principal sites given in this book, and more detailed directions and sketch maps are given for individual locations in each of the Stand Notes. Some of the maps included are reproduced from official histories and should be of assistance in relating events to the ground today, despite the changes which have taken place since.

The Monastery
The Monastery itself is open to visitors from 0830 to 1230 hours, and from 1530 to 1700 hours (1800 hours in Summer) every day. It is well worth visiting, not only for the important part it played in the battle,

The Monastery above Cassino before the bombing.

but in its own right as an important historical and religious building, which has risen from the ashes and destruction of the war years. Visitors are requested to dress and behave in a manner appropriate to a religious community: shorts and scanty clothes are banned from the Monastery, and visitors are advised that the marble floors can be very slippery for the wrong shoes. Anything which might disturb the solemnity of the building, such as flash photography, eating on the premises, and loud conversation, is forbidden. Certain parts may be closed when services are in progress.

Two of the recommended Stands are on Monastery land, and access has to be made through a gate which is normally locked. You are advised to seek advice on this locally, from the Monastery itself or from the Associazone Battaglia di Cassino.

Museums

Until 2004 there was a notable absence of military museums in the area, the nearest being that at Piana del Orme some forty-six kilometres away near Latina, which covers the Italian participation in the Second World War with imagination and contains a great deal of material, including displays on the Cassino Battles. If there is time, it is well worth a visit, as is the museum which has recently been opened in Cassino – The Cassino War Memorial. Details may be found at: "http://www.cassinowarmuseum.it". Still being developed at the time of writing, it has a good display of photographs and cases of uniforms and equipment. The Associazone Battaglia di Cassino is working hard to develop a lasting record as close to the site of the battles as possible. Alessandro Campagna (email alessandrocampagna@libero.it) is responsible for liaison with veterans' associations, and he and his colleagues are most helpful to those seeking more information on the conflict. A difficulty faced by anyone visiting battlefields is that of putting images of people and the paraphernalia of war onto what is today an empty stretch of scenery. Museums assist the observer to conjure up a mental picture of events in the past; as, I hope, will this book.

Accommodation

There are a number of hotels in and around Cassino. I have generally used the Hotel Rocca, on the via Sferracavalli, which is a short distance out of town, close to where 34th (US) Division crossed the Rapido valley towards the range of mountains crowned by Monte Cairo in 1944. The hotel is friendly and has a restaurant. A major plus is the ability of many of the staff to speak English!

Prelude

CASSINO – AN OVERVIEW

Italy September 1943 – The Strategic Situation

By early September 1943 the tide of the war in Europe was flowing in the Allies' favour. The Russians had broken the German hold on Stalingrad as far back as February of that year and were advancing westwards. In the Mediterranean Theatre, the Axis forces had been defeated in North Africa on 13 May, Sicily had been invaded (Operation HUSKY) on 10 July, finally falling on 17 August, and on 3 September the British Eighth Army crossed the Straits of Messina unopposed. Six days later, the US Fifth Army under General Mark Clark landed at Salerno (Operation AVALANCHE), south of Naples, following the announcement of the Italian Armistice.

"ALLIES LAND ON THE MAINLAND OF EUROPE. At 4.30 on the morning of September 3rd, fourth anniversary of the the outbreak of war, 8th Army troops set foot on the main land of Europe. They crossed the Straits of Messina and made an assault landing on the toe of Italy. Within a week of the landing Italy had surrendered unconditionally." Thus announced the news release accompanying this photograph.

At the strategic level Italy had been relegated by the Allies to a secondary role. Never enthusiastic about operations in the Mediterranean Theatre, in May 1943 the Americans let it be known that unless the British whole-heartedly supported their chosen strategy of launching a cross-Channel invasion at the earliest opportunity, then they would give the Pacific Theatre priority. OVERLORD was to take precedence, and operations in Italy would be carried out only to draw German divisions away from France and thereby improve the odds of a successful invasion there. Both the Americans and the Russians saw the opening of the Second Front (by which they meant North-West Europe) as being of paramount importance. Churchill was not wholly in agreement. To him, the 'soft underbelly of Europe' offered the opportunity to weaken the Germans and to lessen the possibility of a failure on the Normandy landing beaches, an event which he was willing to postpone until the prospects were much more favourable. A war of attrition which steadily eroded the enemy was preferable to risking a failure in France which would mean that the Germans could devote their main effort to the Eastern Front, with the possibility of their being able to come to a negotiated peace with the Russians. A failed invasion in 1944 would present the possibility that Germany would be left in control of mainland Europe, that the Americans might withdraw from the war in the west – or even that the atomic bomb's first use might be elsewhere than on Japan; both the Allies and Germany were developing that weapon as quickly as they were able.

The Campaign in Southern Italy

Churchill's views on the risks of OVERLORD were not without strength, but they failed to carry the argument, not least because the other Allies saw his Mediterranean interest as a re-run of his failed Gallipoli strategy during the First World War. Despite his protestations at the Cairo Conference in December 1943, OVERLORD and ANVIL (a landing on the Riviera Coast of France) were to be the supreme operations for the following year. To this end, seven veteran divisions – four American and three British – were to be re-allocated from Italy to OVERLORD, as were most of the landing ships and craft currently in the Mediterranean. This transfer was to be completed by 1 November 1943. Any major amphibious operation in the theatre had to be before this date, a constraint that severely limited the planners' options. Those who held the senior planning appointments were also changed: Eisenhower and Montgomery were themselves tasked with leaving the Mediterranean Theatre to prepare for the invasion of Normandy.

The Italian terrain favoured the German defenders.

Italy – The Operational Difficulties

For the Allied forces in the Mediterranean, the knowledge that they were to become no more than a side-show employing reduced forces to achieve an ill-defined aim, was a situation hardly likely to generate enthusiasm or to achieve dynamic results. The prospect of restricting amphibious operations was serious. The geography of Italy – a long peninsula with a backbone of mountains – presented the invaders with major difficulties and restricted their options. Obvious routes of advance up the leg of the country were defined by the historic roads, which ran along the Tyrrhenian and Adriatic coastlines, separated by the difficult mountain ranges which reached heights of over 9,000 feet; and with river valleys running to the sea on both sides. Progress had to be across a series of natural obstacles on a comparatively narrow front, with no alternative but to grind away at the enemy's defences in frontal attacks. Options of outflanking the Germans depended on the availability of naval forces to enable landings behind their lines, which were firmly anchored on the coastlines and made full use of the terrain. The decision to give priority to OVERLORD and to denude the Mediterranean theatre of amphibious shipping was to reduce the possibilities for the Allies. Airborne forces were likewise to be redeployed to the United Kingdom, removing the potential for

15

'General Mud... comes into action on the Eighth Army front' is how the caption reads on the back of this photograph. Torrential rain fell for several days in the winter of 1943-44.

bypassing the German defences by air.

A few hours driving along the minor roads of the Cassino region will bring home the message about terrain. Understanding the course of a battle is always enhanced by walking the ground, and time spent doing this in Italy is well spent, for map interpretations really do not give the picture at all – and in the war years led to misunderstandings and frustration between those fighting the battles and the armchair strategists in London and Washington, who could not see the difficulty in pushing rapidly ahead.

To the problems presented by the physical features were added

Royal Engineers clear debris during the repair of a blown-up road over a railway tunnel, on an Italian mountainside near Scilla, September 1943.

The cross-country terrain during the summer weather presented its own problems of dryness and dust.

those of the climate. During the summer months, the ground was baked hard, allowing relative freedom of movement for vehicles but bringing the tell-tale signs of clouds of dust whenever they moved, a gift to the ever-vigilant observation posts of the defenders. In winter, rain and snow turned the off-road areas and the small tracks into quagmires, difficult of passage by vehicles and churned into seas of mud by the feet of marching men and the hooves of the mule trains, often the only feasible means of transport. The winter of 1943-44 was the severest of the century thus far, only to be surpassed by that of 1944-45. Never slow to improve upon nature's obstacles, the German defenders destroyed dams and flooded areas of low-lying ground to add to the Allies' problems, and tore up roads and railways that offered causeways through the mud. In the mountains, a few pounds of explosive often sufficed to bar passage by blowing a road into the valley below.

Even the vegetation appeared to conspire against the invader. Tank commanders were to find that olive and vine branches and foliage grew at such a height that they hid anti-tank gunners, who had a relatively unimpeded view of the tanks' hulls from underneath the canopy of leaves.

A Moroccan Goumier of the French Expeditionary Corps. One of the many nationalities in the Allied armies.
Associazone Battaglia di Cassino

As well as the aforementioned difficulties, the Allies had to cope with managing a truly international force, the composition of which illustrates the fact that this was, in reality, a world war. Fighting in Italy were not only Americans and British, but also troops from Poland, France (including Algeria, Morocco and Tunisia), India (present day India, Pakistan and Bangladesh), Nepal, New Zealand, Canada, South Africa, Japanese-Americans from Hawaii, and – at a later date – Brazilians. Cypriots manned some Allied mule trains, and African porters were employed to manhandle supplies. Greek naval vessels were present offshore. Italians fought on both sides of the conflict, some in support of the Allies following the surrender, others faithful to the Fascist cause.

Hairpin bends on Italian mountain roads caused difficulties for trucks towing larger calibre guns.

Narrow roads and axle-deep mud made swift follow-up of the Germans extremely difficult.

Among the German forces were soldiers from Austria and from countries under German domination – Poles and representatives of other eastern European nations were also to be found in their ranks.

Apart from the obvious difficulties of language, and the effect on communication and understanding, this mixture of nationalities presented a diversity of culture, faith and motivation. Dietary requirements and religious sensibilities apart, some Allied contingents had their own particular axes to grind in the battles against the Germans. Both the French and the Poles, for example, felt that they had something to prove, the French seeking to restore their military prestige after the disastrous days of 1940, the Poles on a mission not only to restore their military standing, but to attract international attention and support for their nation's independence once the war was over. The result, for both of these groups, was an almost fanatical determination to succeed, which at times led to a bravery verging on foolhardiness.

Salerno to the Gustav Line
The advance through Italy was bitterly contested. The Germans had responded to Operation AVALANCHE, the Salerno landings, with vigour. The landings were not unexpected – the geographical and operational constraints (a suitable landing beach, close to a port which might be swiftly captured and turned to Allied use, and within

Polish soldiers with the Eighth Army are halted by a blown bridge. Italian women carry on with their washing.

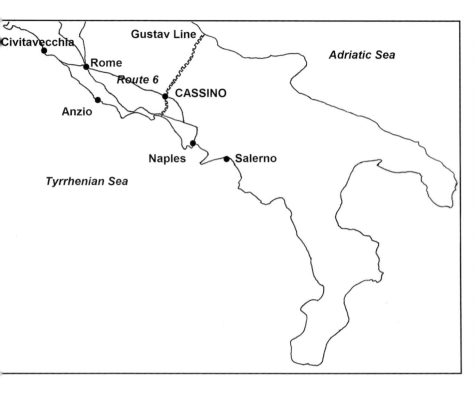

operational range of fighter cover from airfields in Sicily and southern Italy) narrowed the options considerably, and the Germans were able to draw their own conclusions and to make appropriate plans. Fearing a lack of support from their Italian allies, the Germans had taken steps to defend the area themselves. Their suspicions were well founded: the Italian government had negotiated a secret peace settlement with the Allies, but were hoping that it would not be made public without advance warning so that they might take measures to protect themselves from the inevitable German reaction. Eisenhower, however, broadcast the news as the invasion fleet was on the way to Salerno, in the expectation that Italian forces would not resist the landings, a move which took the Italian government by surprise and left them scurrying for cover from their ex-partners in the Axis. Little was achieved by way of lessening the defences – the Germans were well-prepared, and had placed little reliance on assistance from the Italians.

The landings were a close-run thing. The event contributed to the commander of the US Fifth Army, General Mark Clark, distrusting the

British, particularly when the British press lauded Montgomery's Eighth Army for coming to the relief of his beleaguered force, when he had already retrieved the situation. It also influenced his anticipation of likely German actions in response to any future landings, a view which was to have its affect later on, with the unclear aims and consequent outcome of the Anzio landings in 1944.

It was apparent that the Allies lacked a coherent strategy which coordinated the actions of their forces – Montgomery had not been tasked with working in harmony with Clark, and although a two-pronged attack (by Fifth and Eighth Armies) may have appeared sensible in principle, their objectives were drawn up in isolation. This was partly because of a lack of overall direction from Eisenhower, who did not issue a clear directive establishing Rome as the objective until 25 September 1943. This uncertainty of the aims of the campaign, married to the problems of the terrain and the climate, and compounded by the German will to turn the Allies' difficulties to their own advantage, led to a growing despondency amongst the American and British planners. Over and above these factors was the realisation that Italy was very much a secondary theatre, which was to be robbed of men and resources for the main North-West Europe offensive which was to strike into Germany from Normandy.

General Von Vietinghoff, the commander of the German Tenth Army, achieved a withdrawal from the Salerno area without letting his forces become trapped. By 1 October 1943, the Allies had captured Naples, and then faced a series of defensive lines running across the country, based on natural obstacles, which included the Volturno River (crossed by the Allies on 15 October) and the Sangro (crossed on 1 December). Hindered by deteriorating weather conditions, the Allies struggled up the leg of Italy, with Fifth Army on the Tyrrhenian coast and Eighth on the Adriatic. The Canadians captured Ortona, after intensive fighting, on 28 December. Fifth Army struggled onwards until it reached the Gustav Line, some sixty miles from Naples.

The Gustav Line

The Gustav Line ran from the Adriatic Sea across the peninsula through Atina and Cassino, to the Gulf of Gaeta on the Tyrrhenian Sea. The narrow Adriatic coastal plain led nowhere, and between it and Cassino lay the Apennine Mountains, rising to over 9,000 feet and regarded as being impassable during winter. To the west of Cassino lay the Liri River valley, which varied in width from five to seven miles, and which offered an obvious route to Rome; between the valley and the Tyrrhenian Sea were the Aurunci and Lepini Mountains, which were again a major obstacle, particularly in winter.

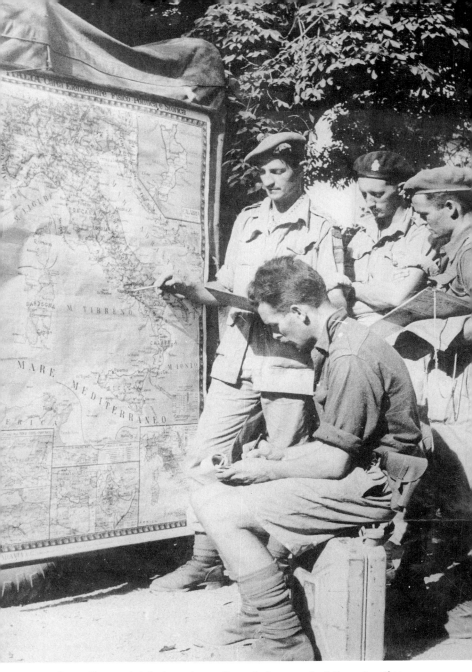

Canadian officers plot their route northwards in pursuit of the retreating Germans. Captain Bob Prince, from Westmount, Quebec points at Naples.

American troops at San Pietro – the fighting before Cassino.
Associazone Battaglia di Cassino

Without adequate shipping to mount a large-scale landing which might bypass the Gustav Line, the solution to the problem of reaching Rome appeared to be the Liri valley. It offered the Allies the possibility of making best use of the mechanised forces available to them, but despite the comparative advantages, formidable obstacles were still to be encountered. In front of the Gustav Line, from north of Cassino to the Gulf of Gaeta, was a series of rivers. The Rapido in the north, the Gari across the Liri valley, and then the Garigliano from the valley down to the Tyrrhenian Sea, were in places over forty yards wide. Additionally, the Liri valley entrance was guarded by two mountain systems. To the south was Monte Maio, nearly 3,000 feet high, which overlooked the Garigliano crossings and the Gari River. North of Cassino was Monte Cairo, 5,000 feet high, with a ridge running to Monte Cassino, 1,500 feet high, atop which sat the Benedictine Monastery.

Between the Monastery and Cassino Town, and protecting the approaches, was Castle Hill, 600 feet high and crowned by the ruins of a medieval castle. A drive down today's Route 430, from Cassino to Minturno, along the Garigliano, shows how strong the position was. A detour off this road to the village

A soldier from 36th (Texas) Division after the attack on San Pietro. The exhaustion is apparent on his face.
Associazone Battaglia di Cassino

The inviting view of the Liri valley from Camino. The mountain in the distance is Monte Caira. Author

of Camino, situated on the western slopes of the mountain of that name (itself the scene of bitter winter fighting in November and December 1943), to look across the Gari valley and up the Liri, will go some way to explaining why Cassino was to prove such a magnet to the Allied planners. After the harsh mountain warfare they had experienced thus far, the flat river valley and the apparently open road to Rome appeared to be a godsend.

For some three months, the Germans had worked to reinforce the natural obstacles which lay before this passage. They had dammed the Rapido River and flooded the river valley north of Cassino, and mined both river banks. Guns, machinegun emplacements and tank turrets had been dug in across the Liri valley entrance, and were reinforced with concrete and steel. The town of Cassino itself had been fortified with pill-boxes, guns and tanks inside reinforced buildings. In the mountains above were gun, mortar and machinegun emplacements, some of which had been blasted out of the solid rock, protected by wire and yet more minefields. The Gustav Line was possibly the strongest and most formidable defensive position in Europe. It was to take the Allies some five months of heavy fighting, some of it in appalling weather conditions, to push through it.

The Monastery before the bombing. Castle Hill in the foreground.

The Battles of Cassino

The Allies identified four separate Battles of Cassino (the Germans counted only three, as they considered the First and Second Battles to be an extension of the same conflict). To confuse matters further, British Army units carry 'Cassino I' and 'Cassino II' as battle honours, which are the two battles for Cassino itself in which British Army formations fought; the First and Fourth Battles appear on the colours under the headings of actions in the surrounding areas – 'Garigliano', 'Liri Valley', and so on. This book will follow the four-battle numbering sequence, as it deals with all of the battles, regardless of the nationalities of the participants.

The First (January 1944) and the last (May) Battles planned to outflank Cassino; Second (February) and Third (March) were frontal attacks on the position, both being preceded by heavy bombing – of the Monastery during the Second, and the town during the Third Battles. First and Fourth Battles included fighting for greater stretches of the Gustav Line; but whereas seven Allied divisions were committed to the first, the equivalent of seventeen were employed in the final battle. The Anzio bridgehead, and the fighting there, was closely linked to the Cassino battles, and it is impossible to consider them in isolation.

Anzio

At Tunis on Christmas Day 1943, the Allied commanders drafted a fresh plan for an amphibious landing south of Rome, codenamed SHINGLE, to take advantage of the German preoccupation with attacks on the Gustav Line. A single-division landing at Anzio had been mooted before, in November 1943, as part of a three-pronged offensive in which the Eighth Army would advance astride Highway 5, followed by a Fifth Army advance up the Liri and Sacco valleys to capture Frosinone. The third phase of this offensive was to have been the Anzio landing, which was intended to link up with the forces from the south. The revised plan now called for two divisions plus some airborne troops and armour to land at Anzio and Nettuno and strike inland towards the Colli Laziali, to block German supply routes and threaten to cut off the Gustav Line defenders. The Allies believed that the Germans lacked sufficient strength to meet attacks on both the Anzio and Gustav Line fronts and would weaken one to reinforce the other. Once this had happened, the advance up the Liri valley could proceed as the enemy was forced to withdraw.

While the landing was still being prepared, Fifth Army began its attack on the Gustav Line. Above Cassino, the French Expeditionary Corps advanced in the mountains in an attempt to turn the German flank on 12 January 1944, and made good, albeit slow progress in the face of determined German resistance. To the south, X (British) Corps attacked across the lower Garigliano between the Gulf of Gaeta and the Liri valley, to

Feldmarschall **Albert Kesselring.**

27

force the other end of the German defences, on 17 January. 5th (British) Division advanced on the coastal sector and 56th (British) Division moved towards Castelforte and the high ground above the Ausente River. By dawn on 18 January the two divisions had pushed ten battalions across the Garigliano. 5th Division was on the Minturno Ridge, with 56th Division troops on either side of Castelforte, when Kesselring ordered *29th* and *90th Panzer Grenadier Divisions*, with elements of the *Herman Goering Panzer Division*, to support the heavily pressed *94th Division*. These units strongly counterattacked X (British) Corps, and although the British held on despite heavy fighting, the Allied hopes of an advance up the Ausente valley and onto the Liri plain were foiled.

Elsewhere on the Gustav Line matters did not go any better. 46th (British) Division's attempt to cross the Garigliano opposite San Ambroglio was abandoned after thick fog stopped all but one company landing on the far bank. The division's task had been to support II (US) Corps' attack further north, where Clark's plan was for 36th (Texas) Division to force crossings over the Gari River (usually – but incorrectly – known as the Rapido River at this spot, and so referred to in American and other histories. The Rapido does not extend this far south) and allow Combat Command B of 1st (US) Armoured Division to pass through into the Liri valley. The attack was a disaster. The 141st Regimental Combat Team (RCT – a formation broadly equivalent in strength to a British brigade) was to cross the Gari north of the village of Sant' Angelo in Theodice, and 143 RCT at two places to the south. Unable to bring the bridging material forward to the river bank because of the minefields, artillery and machinegun fire, and hindered by the flooded ground, the engineers left the infantry to move the equipment themselves. On the night of 20 January, the Americans carried their assault boats to the river in heavy fog and under enemy fire. Although lanes had been marked through the minefield, the tapes were blown aside or destroyed by mortar and artillery fire, and some troops went astray and became casualties to anti-personnel mines. The banks of the river were two to three feet high, the river some nine feet deep, and the water swiftly flowing. Boats were swept away by the current, and by dawn on 21 January only two and a half companies of 141 RCT had crossed the river, and only one of the four footbridges remained. To the south, the 1st Battalion of the 143 RCT managed to cross the river, but was forced back to the east bank. At the Regiment's second crossing site, there was complete confusion and none of the 3rd Battalion got across.

The attack was renewed during the evening and night of 21 January, and 3rd Battalion and two companies from each of the 1st and 2nd

Battalions of 143 RCT managed to cross and establish a bridgehead about 550 yards beyond the far bank, before being forced back again in the morning. Upstream, the 141 RCT got most of two battalions into its small bridgehead, but lost contact with them and were unable to provide reinforcements or supplies. Only a few survivors managed to return. 36th (US) Division suffered 1,681 casualties in its attempt to force the crossing, and by 22 January, the day planned for the Anzio landings, the attacks on the Gustav Line had ground to a halt in the face of German counterattacks. But although the Fifth Army had not pushed its way into the Liri valley, hopes still held that the Germans had committed their reserves and that Operation SHINGLE would break the deadlock.

Anzio 22 January 1944 – Operation SHINGLE

H Hour for SHINGLE was set for 0200 hours on 22 January. As the landing craft hit the beaches, they found no enemy to meet them. Although the Germans expected a landing at some stage, they anticipated that it would be much later in the year, and they were unsure of where it might be. The two divisions due to defend the area had been sent south three days earlier, leaving only skeleton forces: only three engineer companies and *2nd Battalion* of *71st Panzer Grenadier Regiment* covered the coast from the mouth of the Tiber to the Mussolini Canal; in one area a single company was responsible for a nine-mile stretch of coastline. Nor had the Germans any idea that the landings were about to happen.

With virtually no opposition and with calm seas, the Allies faced few problems. VI Corps landed without difficulty, and 3rd (US) Division moved quickly inland and destroyed the bridges on the

American troops landing on their sector of the Anzio beachhead.

Mussolini Canal as part of the plan to establish a defensive perimeter. In the centre the Rangers seized the port of Anzio, which was undamaged apart from Allied bombing, and later in the morning the paratroops occupied Nettuno. Although 1st (British) Division encountered poor beach conditions on the left, by noon on D Day VI Corps had reached all of its immediate objectives, and by early afternoon the port was ready to handle LST's and other shallow-draft craft. By midnight some 36,000 men, 3,200 vehicles and large quantities of stores were ashore. At a cost of thirteen killed, ninety-seven wounded and forty-four captured or missing, the initial landings had succeeded.

German reaction to the landings was to move elements of *4th Parachute* and the *Hermann Goering Divisions* south from the Rome area to block the roads running north from the Alban Hills. The German anti-aircraft commander for Rome was ordered to ring the beachhead with his 88mm guns in an anti-tank role, and within twenty-four hours units were moved from Yugoslavia, France and Germany to reinforce elements of *3rd Panzer Grenadier* and *71st Infantry Divisions* as they moved into the Anzio area. Despite Allied air interference, thousands of German troops concentrated on Anzio. What Kesselring did not do was to move troops from the Gustav Line to contain this new threat, which is what the Allies had wanted. Anzio was to become a problem for them as the ring around the beachhead grew stronger and the

A German 88mm AA gun being employed in an anti-tank role. The antiaircraft guns protecting Rome were brought in to help contain the Anzio beachhead.

Germans began to launch powerful counterattacks. Instead of taking the pressure off the troops on the Gustav Line, the balance swung so that they now had to work to distract the Germans from their operations at Anzio. A disgusted Churchill was later to comment that what he had hoped would be 'hurling a wildcat onto the shore' had become no more than a 'stranded whale', as VI Corps found itself fighting to hold onto the ground it had occupied, rather than striking inland to threaten the German lines of communication to the Gustav Line.

Cassino 24 January – 12 February 1944

After the failure to open the Liri valley, and with X (British) Corps' advance halted on the Garigliano bridgehead, Clark directed his attention to the north of Cassino. The French Expeditionary Corps was to push towards Terelle and Piedimonte. 34th (US) Division would cross the Rapido to the north of Cassino on the left of the French, and attack the mountains north of and behind Monte Cassino.

The Americans attacked on 24 January, across two miles of flooded river valley and into prepared positions defended by minefields and wire. 133 RCT had Points 56 and 213, and the barracks in Cassino, as preliminary objectives. Once these had been taken, 168 RCT was to pass through and attack Monte Castellone, Colle Sant' Angelo and Albaneta Farm. 135 RCT would move southwards and take Cassino town. Despite the obstacles, and the mud which rendered tank support impossible, a small bridgehead was across the river by midnight on 25 January and one company of 135 RCT reached the outskirts of Cassino before being driven back. During the following two days attacks were renewed, and on 29 January engineers succeeded in laying Sommerfield tracks which allowed tanks to cross in strength and support the infantry in taking Points 56 and 213. Two days later, Caira village, which contained the HQ of *131 Grenadier Regiment* was taken.

By the same date, the French had captured Monte Belvedere. They consolidated on a position projecting into the German lines, but could advance no further. Between them and 34th (US) Division, 142 RCT from 36th (US) Division was to move across the mountains to Route 6.

The Americans were now faced not only by the dreadful winter weather but by formidable ground. To their front lay the 2,500-foot high Monte Castellone, from whence a ridge ran southwards to Point 706, splitting into two spurs, one going south-west through Colle Sant' Angelo to Point 575, about 2,000 yards west of Monte Cassino. The second fell to Albaneta Farm. Parallel to the Point 706-575 ridge, another ran from Maiola Hill to Point 593, about 1,000 yards west of the Monastery. This was to become known as Snakeshead Ridge from its

Troops were rushed in to contain the Allied bridgehead at Anzio. German machine gunners pass a Panther on a muddy road in Italy.

appearance on the map. Between Point 593 and the Monastery was a saddle with a central knoll, Point 444. The ground was broken, stony, and cut with crevasses and hollows. Covered with rocks and boulders and patches of scrub, it was impossible to dig trenches in the ground without the aid of explosives – a factor which the Germans had been able to cater for, but which any attacker would find an additional problem.

Despite these circumstances and in the face of strong enemy resistance, the American divisions captured Monte Castellone, Monte Maiola, Point 706 and Point 175 opposite Castle Hill by 3 February. Between 8 and 11 February, they made their final attempts to take the Monastery and Cassino town. Point 593 changed hands three times in as many days, fought for in rain, sleet and snow, but the Germans retained possession. By 12 February the Americans had fought themselves to a standstill, with some companies being reduced to no more than thirty men. Some of the eighteen battalions had lost eighty per cent of their effective strength. When relieved by 4th Indian Division, about fifty Americans had to be carried out by stretcher, being too exhausted by the cold and battle to walk down the slopes; some were killed by German artillery fire in the process.

From the outset, the attacks along the Gustav Line Front had not been strong enough to overcome the defences. Prematurely launched in an attempt to support SHINGLE, they had become a series of attempts to rush the Cassino position without managing to concentrate overwhelming strength at any one point. When the battle ground to a stop in early February, the British had lost over 4,000 men for the cost of a small bridgehead across the Garigliano. The French took 2,500 casualties, and had captured Monte Belvedere. 36th (US) Division had lost 2,000 on the Rapido and above Cassino; and 34th (US) Division 2,200 in establishing a foothold in the mountains overlooking Cassino. Despite the disadvantages of being overlooked on three sides and difficult to re-supply, this foothold offered a possible route to Monte Cassino.

From the German perspective, they had not only held the Allies but had identified weak points in their own defences, which they were now able to strengthen. It might have been reasonable to expect that

Cassino: THE FIRST BATTLE, 30 January to 12 February 1944.

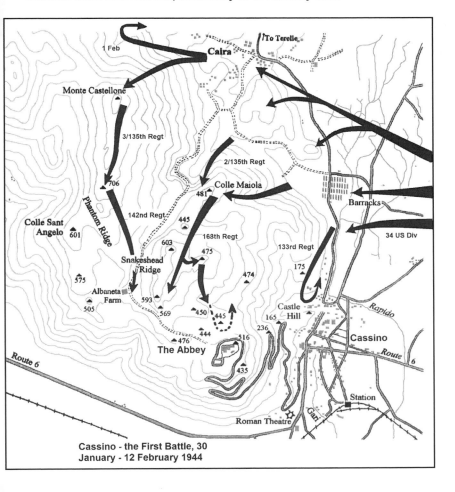

Cassino - the First Battle, 30
January - 12 February 1944

Fallschirmjäger operating an MG 34 while manning the Gustav Line.

the Allies would wait until the weather improved before renewing their attacks, but there were signs that the German *Fourteenth Army* was preparing to open an offensive on Anzio. To draw the Germans' pressure off the beachhead, the next battle for Cassino would be launched very swiftly, and even more prematurely than the first. Rather than the Anzio operation assisting the Cassino attackers, they were now called upon to take the pressure off VI Corps by mounting another offensive.

The New Zealand Corps now took responsibility for the Cassino sector. Consisting of 2nd New Zealand and 4th Indian Divisions, it was commanded by General Freyberg VC. As II (US) Corps had nearly taken the position from the mountains north of the Monastery, it appeared that a further attempt along the same lines might succeed.

Second Cassino

Freyberg's plan was that 4th Indian Division, which was practised in mountain warfare, should capture Monte Cassino while the experienced 2nd New Zealand Division took the town of Cassino from the south east, along the line of the railway. With the river valley flooded, the railway embankment offered a causeway which tanks might cross once the infantry had secured the far end and engineers had cleared any obstacles from it. But this part of the operation was in direct view of Monte Cassino.

Not everyone was convinced that the Germans were not using the Monastery as an observation post or had prepared it for defence, despite their declaration that it was to be regarded as neutral. In the absence of intelligence information on it, General Tuker, GOC 4th Indian Division, researched the Monastery's potential as a fortress in the second-hand bookshops of Naples. Not only did he see it as a physical threat, but he considered it (as did many of the soldiers in the valley below) as a morale-threatening factor which had to be removed before any attack took place. He therefore made strong representations to have it bombed. A contentious issue, it was nevertheless agreed that the bombing should proceed and that – if possible – the Monastery should be levelled. While there may have been valid reasons for this,

Cassino: THE SECOND BATTLE, 15-17 February 1944.

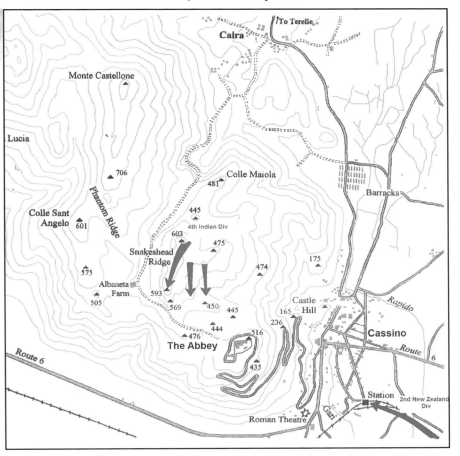

the net result was to ensure that the buildings became a readily defensible strongpoint.

There was little time to move 7 Indian Brigade into position before the attack. The brigade completed its take-over of the American positions on Snakeshead Ridge during the night of 14/15 February, with the bombing timetabled for the 15th. Allied intelligence indicated that the Germans would attack at Anzio at some date not earlier than 16 February, and the Allied Air Forces would be needed there. Any air involvement at Cassino had to be before that date, which gave only a bare minimum of time for the ground plan to be finalized and the troops positioned to carry it out.

On arriving on Snakeshead Ridge, 1st Battalion the Royal Sussex Regiment found that, contrary to expectations, Point 593 was not in friendly hands but was still firmly held by the enemy. With it being necessary to capture this position before attacking the Monastery, and as this could not be done successfully in daylight, the decision was taken that this preliminary operation would take place twelve hours after the bombing, during the night of 15/16 February, despite the respite that the delay would give the defenders.

At 0925 hours on the morning of the 15th, the bombing started. In an operation that lasted until 1332 hours, 135 Fortresses and eighty-seven Mitchells and Marauders dropped a total of 443 tons of bombs on the Monastery. Although the outer walls were breached in several places, these gaps did not extend from top to bottom, and the ruins were quickly fortified by the Germans. Nor did the bombing assist the Allied ground forces – many of them had not been pre-warned and were unprepared for it to happen. In particular, the New Zealanders tasked to make the attack along the railway line were not yet in a position to start their advance.

With little time for preparation and restricted by the narrowness of Snakeshead Ridge, the Royal Sussex' attack on Point 593 was carried out by one company. Too close to the enemy for artillery support, and without mortars because the ammunition had been lost, C Company advanced in the darkness. It came under intense machinegun fire and showers of grenades after moving forward some fifty yards. Short of their own grenades, which were essential weapons in this rocky terrain, it proved impossible to advance further, and the company withdrew before dawn, having suffered casualties of two officers and thirty-two men killed or wounded out of the three and sixty-three that had opened the attack.

The following night, 16/17 February (the night of the German counteroffensive at Anzio), the entire battalion renewed the attack. Some men of D Company reached Point 593, but were driven off by the

Gurkhas in Italy.

defenders from 3 *Parachute Regiment*. The battalion withdrew again, having taken casualties of ten officers and 130 men killed, wounded or taken prisoner from the twelve and 250 that had advanced earlier in the night.

The New Zealand Corps was now ready to make the attack which had been originally planned to follow the bombing of the Monastery, advancing along the railway line into the town of Cassino to capture the railway station. This was to complement yet another attempt in the mountains above, where 4/6 Rajputana Rifles were to capture Point 593 and then exploit to Point 444, which lay a few hundred yards below the Monastery. To the battalion's left, 1/9 Gurkhas were to attack 444 directly across a gully running down from Snakeshead, and 1/2 Gurkhas, further left again, had the Monastery itself as their objective.

At midnight on 17/18 February, the Rajputanas advanced on Point 593, to be halted about 100 yards short of the objective by machinegun and mortar fire, and showers of grenades. Despite the failure to take the Point, 1/9 Gurkhas moved off towards Point 444 at 0215 hours. They, too, were stopped by intense fire from 593 after moving about 300 yards, and had worked to their right, towards the Rajputanas, in attempting to deal with it. Neither unit could take the Point.

On the left, 1/2 Gurkhas went on through the ravine towards the Monastery. Running into what they had believed from aerial photographs to be no more than a belt of scrub, they found it to be

The Monastery after the bombing. Polish Institute

Following the bombing of the Monastery by the Allies German troops were able to move in and use the ruins as a fortress. *Fallschirmjäger* **are seen setting up mortars protected from counter fire by the partially demolished walls.**

Observation in and around the ruined Monastry greatly assisted the defenders.

heavily wired and mined, and they, too, came under attack. Half of the leading platoons were cut down by mines, the remainder by machinegun fire and grenades, and the following companies were prevented from advancing by the crossfire. The CO was among the wounded. Despite this resistance, a small party of Gurkhas was later reported to have fought its way right to the walls of the Monastery before being killed. Some months later, a captured German paratroop officer claimed to have led a counter-attack which cleared Gurkhas from within the building itself. If true, they were the first Allied soldiers to have penetrated it; and the last to do so until May that year. Three battalions were now pinned down and had to be extricated before daybreak.

In the valley below, 28 New Zealand (Maori) Battalion advanced along the railway embankment on a two-company front. They were followed by sappers to clear mines and to build Bailey Bridges across the Rapido and a canal to allow tanks to cross, a task which should have been completed by dawn to provide support for the infantry. To give the maximum time for this, the advance started soon after dark. Under continuous mortar fire and through mines and wire, one Maori company took the station, but the other found themselves blocked by a twenty-foot ditch in front of their objective, a group of mounds known as the 'Hummocks' 300 yards south of the engine shed. Sappers began to remove the mines, having also had to move the railway track, which – being iron - interfered with the detectors. By daybreak they had cleared the embankment and laid one bridge, but the second was incomplete. This left the infantry at the end of the embankment, unsupported by tanks or anti-tank guns. General Kippenberger, GOC 2nd New Zealand Division, decided to screen the station from observation from the Monastery by a day-long smokescreen, which would require some 30,000 smoke shells – which the RASC fetched from Naples, seventy miles away. Soon after 1500 hours, German tanks and infantry were heard advancing through the smoke (a double-edged weapon which covered their movements from the Allied artillery) from two directions, and the Maoris were thrown back. Of a force numbering some 200, 130 had become casualties. The battle was over, with the solitary gain of a bridge over the Rapido.

Third Cassino
18 February, the day that the battle was brought to a stop, was also the climax of the Anzio battle, when the tide began to turn against the German counterattacks. With less pressure on Anzio, Allied attention was now concentrated on the Cassino problem. Having attempted to outflank the position to the south by a river crossing, and to the north via the mountains, the next option was to try the centre. Freyberg's plan was straightforward: to capture the town from the north and secure the river crossings for an advance up the Liri valley. Following the bombing of Cassino town, the attack was to be made down Caruso Road, the Parallel Road, and the Pasquale Road, all of which met in the bottleneck of the town. New Zealanders would capture the town, with a company detached to take Castle Hill. A second battalion would assist in mopping up the town, and a third would come down Pasquale Road and move through on to the station. All this was to take place during the afternoon after the bombing.

In the evening the Indian Brigade would take over the Castle and use it as a jumping-off point for their attack on the Monastery. Castle Hill stands on the slopes, astride a saddle linking it with Monastery

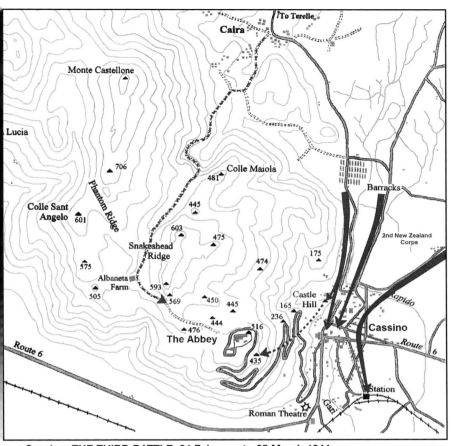

Cassino: THE THIRD BATTLE, 24 February to 25 March 1944.

Hill (and the reason for the Castle's existence). Points 165 and 236 on the road made a defensive position, and were the Indian's second objective. Point 435 (Hangman's Hill) made a possible FUP for the final assault on the Monastery.

The preparations for the bombing were completed by 24 February; but then the weather deteriorated and flying became impossible for the next three weeks. Codenamed Operation DICKENS, the bombing plan required three clear days of dry weather for flying and to firm up the ground for tanks. On the mountains, 4th Indian Division held on to their exposed sangars and scrape-holes in freezing, rain-sodden conditions, while the New Zealanders on the edges of the town maintained an existence in their soaking holes in the valley. The New Zealanders suffered 263 casualties in one brigade, and the Indians a similar number, in this period.

During this three-week lull the Germans carried out reliefs, placing the entire Monte Cassino feature and town in the hands of *1st Parachute Division*. The town itself was turned into a strongpoint in which tanks and pillboxes were built into the rubble of buildings. The Hotels Continental and des Roses, and a palazzo, made particularly tough nests on the western side of the town. Many of these defences were connected by tunnels, and the area was thickly sown with mines: half a million were cleared after the fighting.

With a clearing of the weather, the attack was scheduled for 15 March. The New Zealand troops, less small groups whose task it was to maintain the deception that there was little different happening, withdrew to a safe distance from the town under cover of darkness. From 0830 to 1200 hours, 455 aircraft dropped 992 tons of high explosive on the town, this time with less than pin-point accuracy. Some aircraft, flying from as far away as England and North Africa, mistook targets and bombed the village of Venafro, some fifteen miles away, and General Leese's caravan at Eighth Army HQ was destroyed. Ninety-six Allied soldiers and 140 civilians were killed. However, no building was left intact in Cassino, where – against all odds – half of the *2nd Battalion* of *3 Parachute Regiment* survived and prepared to defend themselves against the attack that they knew would follow.

At noon, the artillery barrage opened. Over 195,000 rounds were fired from 890 Allied guns, on and around Cassino town, until 2000 hours. 25 NZ Battalion moved off from their start line, 1,500 yards

British engineers prepare a crossing in support of those fighting for Cassino.

north of the town as the barrage opened, with the immediate objective of a line along Route 6. Led by tanks, they moved on either side of Caruso Road, with more tanks on the Parallel Road. Met by heavy machinegun, small-arms and mortar fire when they reached the prison on the edge of the town, their advance slowed as they fought their way from crater to crater amongst the destroyed buildings. One company reached the area of the Convent, on the northern branch of Route 6, at dusk, but with very little support from the tanks of 19 NZ Armoured Regiment, which could make but poor progress through the piles of rubble. 26 NZ Battalion stood by in support, but was not called forward.

Meanwhile, the detached company took the Castle and the lower hairpin bend on the road, taking forty-four prisoners and killing several Germans at a cost of six killed and fifteen wounded.

As darkness fell, 26 NZ Battalion moved forward. But torrential rain started to fall, filling the craters and plunging the area into blackness. The troops had to hang on to each other's belts to find their way. Too few troops had been fed into the town during the hours of daylight to take full advantage of the bombing, and now the sappers were being hindered in their mine- and obstacle-clearing operations by the wet and dark. As the night wore on, the New Zealanders moved a total of three battalions into the town and its outskirts.

Throughout the night of 15/16 March, operations continued on the hillsides above the town. By 0300 hours 1/4 Essex Regiment had relieved the New Zealanders on Castle Hill and captured Point 165, a hairpin bend about 300 yards away on the road leading to the Monastery, which was to form a firm base for the Indian attack further along the hillside. 1/6 Rajputana Rifles were to move through for the next stage of the operation, and take Point 236 (on the bend above 165) followed by 1/9 Gurkhas, who in turn were to move onto Hangman's Hill. Dispersed by enemy artillery fire, which caused several casualties in two of their companies which then got lost for the rest of the night, the Rajputs succeeded in taking their objective with the other two companies. They were then driven off by German counterattacks, and the survivors withdrew to the area of the Castle.

Waiting unsuccessfully until 0200 hours for news of the Rajputs, the Gurkhas proceeded with their attack regardless. Using different tracks, two companies advanced. One company was blocked by the Germans, the other lost contact with the battalion and disappeared. At 0245, one Rajput company made another unsuccessful attack on Point 236, and both companies tried again at dawn, with the same result. Battalion HQ was knocked out by mortar fire, the CO and adjutant both becoming casualties, and the companies again withdrew to the Castle.

On the morning of 16 March, supported by fire from tanks which could not yet enter the town, the New Zealanders were involved in street fighting. News of C Company 1/9 Gurkha Rifles arrived, to say that it had taken its objective and was on Hangman's Hill. The Indians had therefore taken their second objective before the first, which left the approach to Hangman's Hill exposed to fire from the hairpin bends. That night the Rajputs again attempted to take Point 236, and provided a diversion under cover of which the remaining Gurkha companies moved between the fighting on the slopes and that in the town onto Hangman's Hill, arriving just in time to see off a German counterattack.

26 NZ Battalion, now led by tanks, captured Cassino station and the Hummocks the next day. They also attacked the Continental Hotel, without success, from the direction of the hillside. The Germans, however, had managed to move more troops back into the town and onto the slopes above Castle Hill.

During the night of 17 March, two companies of 4/6 Rajputana Rifles moved supplies up to the Gurkhas on Hangman's Hill, but were cut off and had to remain with them. Hereafter, supplies were dropped by air, although most missed and ended up in enemy hands.

A major effort was planned for 19 March. 28 (Maori) Battalion would attack the Continental Hotel, and the Gurkhas and 1/4 Essex would attack the Monastery from Hangman's Hill. The Essex had to move from the Castle across the slopes to Hangman's by 0600 hours, handing their positions over to 4/6 Rajputanas. Up the 'impossible' Cavandish Road which ran around the rear of the Monastery position, a tank attack was to be made, with the intention of drawing German attention away from the assault coming from Hangman's Hill.

Shortly after two Essex companies began to move out of the Castle at 0500 hours the Germans launched a counterattack on it, catching the Essex and Rajput companies on the hairpin bend at Point 165 and pushing through them to the foot of the Castle walls. The Essex companies were ordered by radio to continue to Hangman's to join the Gurkhas, whose attack was now postponed. Moving through German fire, only seventy of the Essex arrived, thirty of whom were wounded. The Germans made three attacks on the Castle, which were repelled by two companies of the Essex and one of 4/6 Rajputanas.

On the Cavendish Road the tank force, consisting of forty Shermans and Stuarts from 20 NZ Armoured Regiment, 7 Indian Infantry Brigade and 760 US Tank Battalion, but with no infantry, attacked Albaneta Farm behind Snakeshead Ridge. They initially subdued the paratroopers' fire from Points 593 and 575 and got to within 1,000 yards of the Monastery, but could not proceed further without infantry support. At 1730 hours they were recalled, having lost six tanks destroyed and another sixteen damaged.

With it proving impossible to mount the attack from Hangman's Hill, a failed tank attack, and no progress on the Continental, the operation was called off on 23 March. When General Wilson suggested a final push, Freyberg replied 'Passchendaele' and Alexander agreed. The Gurkha, Rajput and Essex companies were withdrawn from the Hill. The Third Battle for Cassino was over.

On 22 February, General Alexander had redefined the strategy for the Italian campaign: 'to force the enemy to commit the maximum number of divisions in Italy at the same time as the cross-Channel invasion is launched.' To ensure this, the Germans had to be drawn into battle and destroyed. That Alexander had already decided that an Army Group offensive was necessary to break the German line rendered Third Cassino all the more futile – the troops deployed were not regarded as being sufficient, even before the battle was joined.

In the two battles the New Zealanders suffered 1,600 casualties (sixty-three officers and over 800 men in the Third Battle), the Indian Division over 3,000 (sixty-five officers and over 1,000 men in the Third).

The Allies now had to consolidate. 78th Division took over the mountain sector and 1 Guards Brigade the town. For the time being, 4th Indian Division had ceased to be a fighting formation.

New Zealanders with captured *Fallschirmjäger* at Cassino.

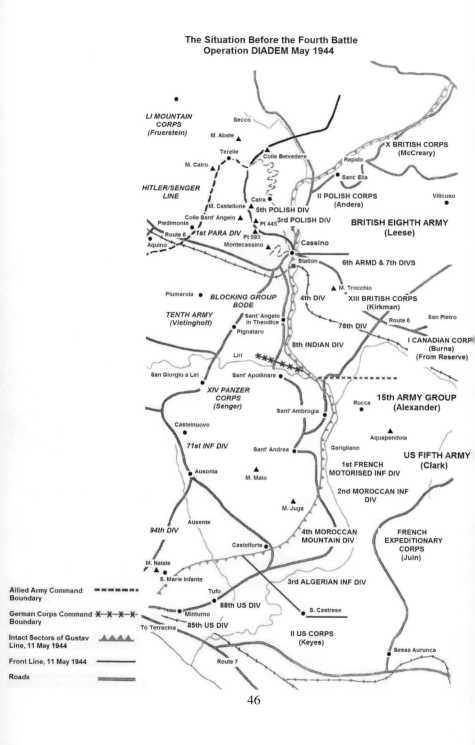

The Situation Before the Fourth Battle
Operation DIADEM May 1944

LI MOUNTAIN CORPS (Fruerstein)

Secco

M. Abate

Terelle

M. Cairo

Colle Belvedere

X BRITISH CORPS (McCreary)

Rapido

Sant' Elia

HITLER/SENGER LINE

M. Castellone

Caira

II POLISH CORPS (Anders)

Viticuso

Colle Sant' Angelo

5th POLISH DIV

Piedimonte

3rd POLISH DIV

Pt 445

BRITISH EIGHTH ARMY (Leese)

Route 6

1st PARA DIV

Pt 593

Aquino

Montecassino

Cassino

Station

6th ARMD & 7th DIVS

Piumarola

BLOCKING GROUP BODE

M. Trocchio

4th DIV

XIII BRITISH CORPS (Kirkman)

TENTH ARMY (Vietinghoff)

Sant' Angelo in Theodice

Pignataro

78th DIV

Route 6

San Pietro

8th INDIAN DIV

I CANADIAN CORP (Burns) (From Reserve)

Liri

San Giorgio a Liri

Sant' Apollinare

XIV PANZER CORPS (Senger)

Sant' Ambrogia

Rocca

15th ARMY GROUP (Alexander)

Casteinuovo

71st INF DIV

Sant' Andrea

Aquapendola

Garigliano

US FIFTH ARMY (Clark)

Ausonia

M. Maio

1st FRENCH MOTORISED INF DIV

2nd MOROCCAN INF DIV

M. Juga

94th DIV

Ausente

4th MOROCCAN MOUNTAIN DIV

FRENCH EXPEDITIONARY CORPS (Juin)

Castelforte

M. Natale

S. Marie Infante

3rd ALGERIAN INF DIV

Tufo

88th US DIV

S. Castrese

Minturno

To Terracina

85th US DIV

II US CORPS (Keyes)

Sessa Aurunca

Route 7

Allied Army Command Boundary

German Corps Command Boundary

Intact Sectors of Gustav Line, 11 May 1944

Front Line, 11 May 1944

Roads

46

Fourth Cassino

Under Operation DIADEM Alexander's staff had planned a regrouping of the Allied forces; Eighth Army was to take over the Cassino and Liri valley sector, where it was to concentrate divisions brought across from the Adriatic and from those British formations in the Garigliano bridgehead. The latter sector was to become the responsibility of two American divisions and the French Expeditionary Corps, which would be reinforced with extra formations before the offensive opened. Placing the French, who were organised and equipped by the Americans, and the Poles with the British, who were likewise responsible for their support, brought a degree of rationalisation to what had been a somewhat haphazard system.

To achieve the desired three-to-one superiority of numbers locally, a major deception plan was necessary. The overall Allied strength at the time was the equivalent of twenty-three divisions to the Germans' eighteen. Alexander therefore made plans to concentrate the equivalent of seventeen divisions, eight from the US Fifth Army and nine from the British Eighth Army, into the twenty miles of front between the Gulf of Gaeta and Cassino.

II Polish Corps was to capture the mountains north of Cassino and the Monastery. XIII (British) Corps, comprising the British 4th, 78th and 6th Armoured Divisions, and 8th Indian Division, was to force the entrance to the Liri valley. I Canadian Corps (1st Canadian Infantry and 5th Canadian Armoured Divisions) and 6th South African Armoured Division were in reserve to exploit up the Liri valley.

To the south, II (US) Corps, comprising 85th and 88th (US) Divisions, and the French Expeditionary Corps, comprising 1st Motorized,

Lieutenant General A F Harding, Alexander's Chief of Staff. The detailed planning of the deception plan laid the foundation for the success of Operation DIADEM.

2nd and 4th Moroccan, and 3rd Algerian Divisions and some 12,000 native Moroccan mountain troops, were to attack through the Aurunci Mountains and the sea. 36th (Texas) Division was in Fifth Army reserve.

In addition to the above-mentioned forces, the Allies had VI Corps in Anzio. By the time they were to play their part in the DIADEM plan, there would be seven full divisions there (1st and 5th British; 3rd, 34th, 36th, 45th and 1st (US) Armoured) plus 1 Special Service Force. Alexander intended that these formations would break out from the

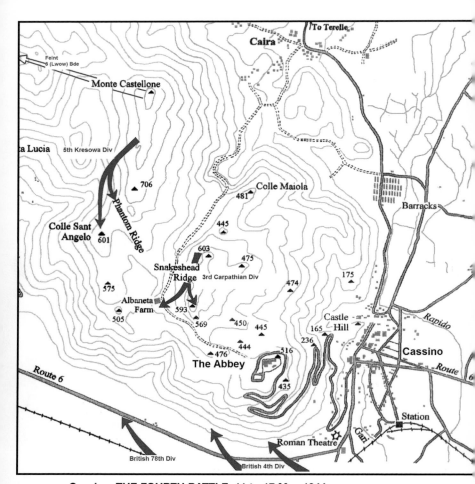

Cassino: THE FOURTH BATTLE, 11 to 17 May 1944.

beachhead to cut off the supply routes and avenue of withdrawal of the German forces on the Gustav Line. With them firmly on Route 6, behind the German *Tenth Army*, a sizable part of that formation would be encircled. The capture of Rome was of secondary importance, and would follow naturally after the planned defeat of the enemy south of the city.

Facing the Allies on the Gustav Line were *44th Infantry Division* and *1st Parachute Division* in the Cassino area, with a regiment from *15th Panzer Division* and a regimental group from *305th Infantry Division* in the Liri valley. *94th Infantry Division* were in the Aurunci Mountains, and *71st Infantry Division* with three battalions from *44th Division* under

48

command were in the coastal sector. The rest of *15th Panzer Division* was in reserve near the coast, and there were elements of *90th Panzer Division* in the German *Tenth Army* Reserve.

The deception plan involved letting the Germans believe that yet another coastal landing was planned behind their lines, this time at Civitavecchia, north of Rome. This was rehearsed in the Bay of Naples by 36th (US) Division, with every suggestion that the Canadian Corps would be part of the operation. In fact, that formation was moved under conditions of great secrecy to the Cassino Front. This element of the plan succeeded in tying up two German divisions at Civitavecchia, one of them armoured. A further two German armoured divisions were placed in reserve at Anzio ready to meet a new landing in that area. The deception plan also called for all movement near the front to be carried out in the hours of darkness, and for stretches of road to be hidden from view by camouflage screens. Dummy tanks and vehicles were used, and British operators manned the Polish radio sets to conceal the fact their forces were in the Cassino area.

In the six weeks between the end of the Third Battle on 24 March and 22 May, helped by improved weather which dried out the tracks, 1,600 guns and 2,000 tanks were assembled between Cassino and the Tyrrhenian Sea. The deception plan had succeeded – as late as the second day of the battle, Kesselring believed that his four divisions on the Cassino front were facing six Allied ones, instead of the thirteen that were actually there. On the Garigliano bridgehead they faced four French divisions, rather than the solitary one they believed to be there.

At 2300 hours on 11 May 1,600 guns opened their fire programme, and during the following four hours all four of the Allied corps began the attack. II (US) Corps on the coastal strip made little progress at first, but the French Expeditionary Corps made impressive gains in the mountains. Not only did it take its objectives during the first four hours, but General Juin pushed 1st French Motorized Division through and to the right, to roll up the German defences towards the Liri valley. At the valley entrance, XIII (British) Corps attacked across the Gari River. 8th Indian Division put two bridges over the river by 0800 hours on 12 May, south of Sant' Angelo, and was able to get tanks across. However, 4th (British) Division was unable to get a bridge in place when they crossed to the north, and without it they had to ferry ammunition over the river, losing thirty-five of their forty boats by 0800. Unable to expand its bridgehead, all but two companies of 28 Brigade were forced back to the eastern bank by evening.

North of Cassino, the Poles attacked Point 593 from Snakeshead Ridge with a brigade from the Carpathian Division, while a brigade from the Kresowa Division attacked Phantom Ridge and Colle Sant'

Angelo. Rather than move on to the Monastery from 593, the advance would go on to Albaneta Farm, leaving the Monastery to be dealt with later. By dawn Poles were on Point 593 and Phantom Ridge to the right, but both brigades had taken heavy casualties and were under constant fire. Unable to supply them, the decision was taken to pull them back during the afternoon.

Despite fighting with great determination, the German defenders could not stand against such odds for long. 12 May was a day of attrition. More bridges were pushed across the river, and on 13 May the German right wing began to give way under American attacks. By 15 May the French captured Monte Maio and Ausonia. On the same day, 78th (British) Division crossed the river and the next day they attacked to turn the defences of Cassino, with the Canadians on their left and 6th Armoured Division in support; the Poles attacked again in the mountains on 17 May and took S Angelo Hill and Point 593, and made the link with 78th Division two miles west of Cassino in the early hours of 18 May. The CO of the British battalion concerned nominated three corporals, all holders of the MM, to make the journey and convey the compliments of the 78th to the Poles. Outflanked, the defenders of the Monastery withdrew, and at 1020 hours the Poles occupied it. The battles for Cassino were over.

Two weeks after the opening of DIADEM, everything was going to plan. Eighth Army, supported by the Fifth, had forced through the Gustav and Adolf Hitler Lines. *Tenth Army* was retreating, and General

Under interrogation a German soldier divulges more than his rank, name and number to an officer of 3rd (US) Division.

Polish troops entering the ruins of the Monastry 18 May 1944.

Truscott's VI Corps was moving to cut it off. *Fourteenth Army* was about to be severely mauled. On 25 May, Truscott's troops were within a day of being across the main German line of withdrawal at Valmontone; but at this stage Clark ordered him to change direction and head northwest to Rome. 3rd (US) Infantry Division, the Special Service Force and part of the Armoured Division were to continue and block Route 6, but the remainder of VI Corps' American formations (34th , 45th, and the newly arrived 36th Divisions, with most of the armour) were to strike up Route 7, directly to the capital.

To the east of VI Corps were the remnants of *362nd* and *715th Divisions*, plus elements of the *Herman Goering* and *92nd Divisions* moving into the Valmontone corridor. To the west were *4th Parachute*, *65th* and *3rd Panzer Grenadier Divisions*, all of which had been restored to almost full strength, and which could – and did – fall back on the Caesar Line which protected Rome. The German forces around Valmontone were sufficient to stop the reduced American force from achieving its objective; and the VI Corps attack up Route 7 was stopped cold. The portion of the line which Clark had decided to attack was in fact the strongest.

General Alexander.

The decision to change VI Corps' axis of attack left the Valmontone route open for the German *Tenth Army* to retire up the Liri. Having originally ordered that his forces should contest every yard of the way up the valley, Kesselring grew increasingly concerned about the American thrust which threatened to cut them off, and unaware that Clark had changed VI Corps' objectives, he withdrew *Tenth Army* to link up with the *Fourteenth*. A series of four blocking points were established to delay the Allies before the Caesar Line. These were to give the Germans more time to develop the more northerly Caesar Line positions.

Morale had completely broken down in some German units, and some of those retreating in front of Eighth Army were only too keen to surrender. Nonetheless, the picture was not the same everywhere. The Germans put up stiff resistance against both Eighth and Fifth Armies. Nor did the terrain help the attackers. One of the reasons for persisting with the Cassino attacks had been the belief that armoured units would be able to sweep up the Liri valley; in the event, they were unable to move only slowly and in small groups, across tributaries, stone banks and terraces, all being made best use of by the defenders. Mines, booby-traps, demolitions and ambushes, as well as defended positions, all served to delay the Allied advance.

There was yet another reason why the Allies' advance was not as swift as had been hoped. To ensure that Eighth Army was sufficiently strong to move up the Liri valley, five divisions (78th British, 8th Indian, 6th British Armoured, 1st Canadian and 1st Canadian Armoured) were pushed into the entrance. The roads were simply not capable of handling the amount of traffic that struggled for position, and inevitable jams and bottlenecks emerged. Supplies were unable to reach their destinations, lorried infantry could not be deployed quickly enough, and armour was often unable to keep up with the infantry on foot. There were tens of thousands of vehicles of all descriptions jostling for position. At one stage, 6th South African Armoured Division's attempt to relieve 1st Canadian Armoured, merely added to the problem by adding yet further numbers of vehicles to what had become a largely immobile mass. The night of 1/2 June saw the worst jam of all as Eighth Army's artillery attempted to move forward.

The lack of pressure on the retreating Germans from both VI Corps and Eighth Army greatly assisted their extraction from the trap that had been intended for them at Valmontone. A lack of urgency seemed to pervade Alexander's headquarters, and Eighth Army's boundary with the French on their left became overstretched as the French forged ahead of the British. Juin's solution was to re-define the inter-corps boundary to allow his forces to cross Route 6 and hopefully block the Germans' escape, but the order for this did not materialise from the British commander. International rivalry, in the push to be at the forefront when Rome fell, seemed to be raising its head again. Clark and Juin appeared convinced that Alexander was manoeuvring to ensure that Eighth Army played its part in taking this prestigious objective. Alexander, on the other hand, was less than impressed with Clark's decision to redefine VI Corps' objective, in what was seen to many to be nothing more than a bid for the Americans to take the prize

General Mark Clark pushed for the City of Rome to become its liberator. His decision allowed the German Tenth Army to withdraw in good order.

Allied vehicles cram the roads.

city, even if this line of action was to allow the German Army off lightly.

Pressure was also being brought by Churchill, who was becoming increasingly dismayed by the prospect of the *Tenth Army* escaping. He signalled Alexander to suggest that the stalled armoured divisions be moved to Anzio via Route 7 so that they might add weight to the Valmontone attack. But the ground did not support sweeping armoured warfare in the way that had been practised in North Africa. There was not enough room for armoured units to deploy, nor were the roads capable of bearing all of the armour's supply columns without disrupting everyone else.

Alexander's refusal to change the Army boundaries appeared to give Clark a fresh interest in Valmontone. Belatedly, at the end of May he decided that II Corps, with additional formations, would attack northwards to cut Route 6 and stop its use by the enemy. This was to take place on 31 May, in conjunction with VI Corps again striking up Route 7. To achieve this, he had to break through the Alban Hills, where *I Parachute Corps* had been reinforced with whatever troops could be found. These included the remnants of *362nd Division*.

The German defences, however, had a weak point. On Monte Artemisio *I Parachute* and *LXXVI Panzer Corps* had their mutual boundary, on a three-mile stretch of thinly held front which was believed to be impenetrable. Although the local commanders were aware of this weakness, they had few troops to remedy it and little was done. 36th (US) Division discovered the gap and broke through it on the night of 30/31 May. This news persuaded Alexander to allow II Corps and the French to cross Route 6, and Clark launched a two-pronged attack on Rome. 85th and 88th (US) Divisions pushed forward to the northwest of Valmontone, astride Route 6, while 36th Division moved along Route 7, to threaten the rear of Lanuvio. On 2 June, *Fourteenth Army's* resistance broke, and the following day *LXXVI Panzer Corps*, followed by *I Parachute Corps*, fell back. On the same day Kesselring obtained Hitler's permission to evacuate Rome, and on 3 June the final rearguards left the Alban Hills. By midnight on 4 June Fifth Army had control of the centre of the city.

But *Army Group C* had survived, and *Tenth Army* had managed to extricate most of its forces. Beyond Rome lay the Trasimene Line, and then the Arno, Gothic, Ghengis Khan, Po, Adige and Alpine Lines. From the Allied viewpoint, the Italian operations – unsatisfactory in some respects as they had been – had tied down German divisions that were not available for use either on the Eastern Front or in Normandy, where their presence might have turned to tide in the close-run battles to secure a foothold in Northwest Europe.

Grave of a German paratrooper. Most burials were more perfunctory affairs. Polish Institute

VISITING THE BATTLEFIELD

With four battles taking place in the same area, over a period of five months, it is difficult to set a route that illustrates them sequentially without having to retrace your steps, sometimes several times. Point 593 would have to be visited four times, for example – once for the Americans, then the Indian Brigade, for a perspective on the tank attack up the Cavendish Road, and finally for the Poles in the final battle. The route outlined opposite enables you to tour the battlefield in a single circuit, with as little repetition as possible. To make sense of the flow of the fighting, it is recommended that you spend a little while reading through this volume before you set out on your journey. Otherwise, the battles can become a blur and confusion ensue – which is not inappropriate, because most of the participants remember them as being just like that!

In planning your trip, do remember that the Monastery closes for a period each day, when the monks are attending their religious devotions. Entrance to both the Monastery and its grounds (which include Point 593 and Albaneta Farm) is not possible then, although it is sometimes possible to get the key to the grounds before the hour of closing, and to return it afterwards. You are advised to seek local advice on this.

German-eye view from Monastery Hill.

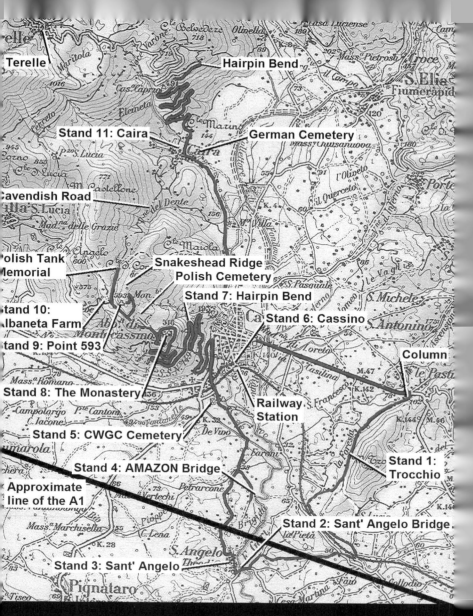

Terelle

Hairpin Bend

Stand 11: Caira

German Cemetery

Cavendish Road

Polish Tank
Memorial

Snakeshead Ridge
Polish Cemetery

Stand 7: Hairpin Bend

Stand 10:
Ibaneta Farm

Stand 6: Cassino

Column

Stand 9: Point 593

Stand 8: The Monastery

Railway
Station

Stand 5: CWGC Cemetery

Stand 1:
Trocchio

Stand 4: AMAZON Bridge

Approximate
line of the A1

Stand 2: Sant' Angelo Bridge

Stand 3: Sant' Angelo

Stands: The numbered locations refer to the relevant chapters in
the following text, where a narrative of the main historical events at

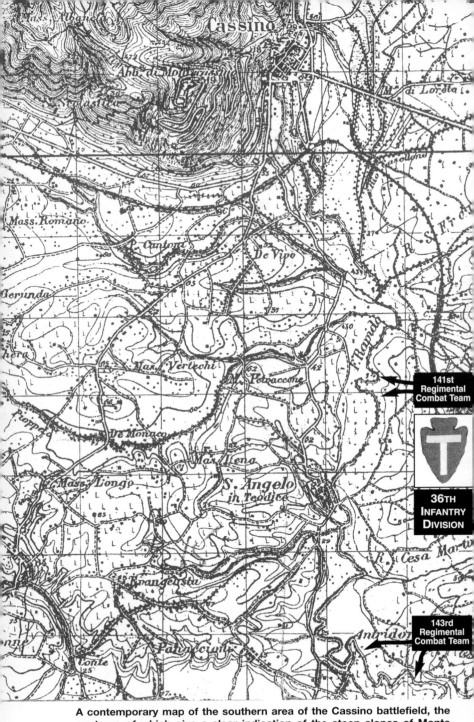

141st Regimental Combat Team

36TH INFANTRY DIVISION

143rd Regimental Combat Team

A contemporary map of the southern area of the Cassino battlefield, the contours of which give a clear indication of the steep slopes of Monte Cassino and Trocchio. The Texas Division's attempted crossing points of the River Gari are indicated.

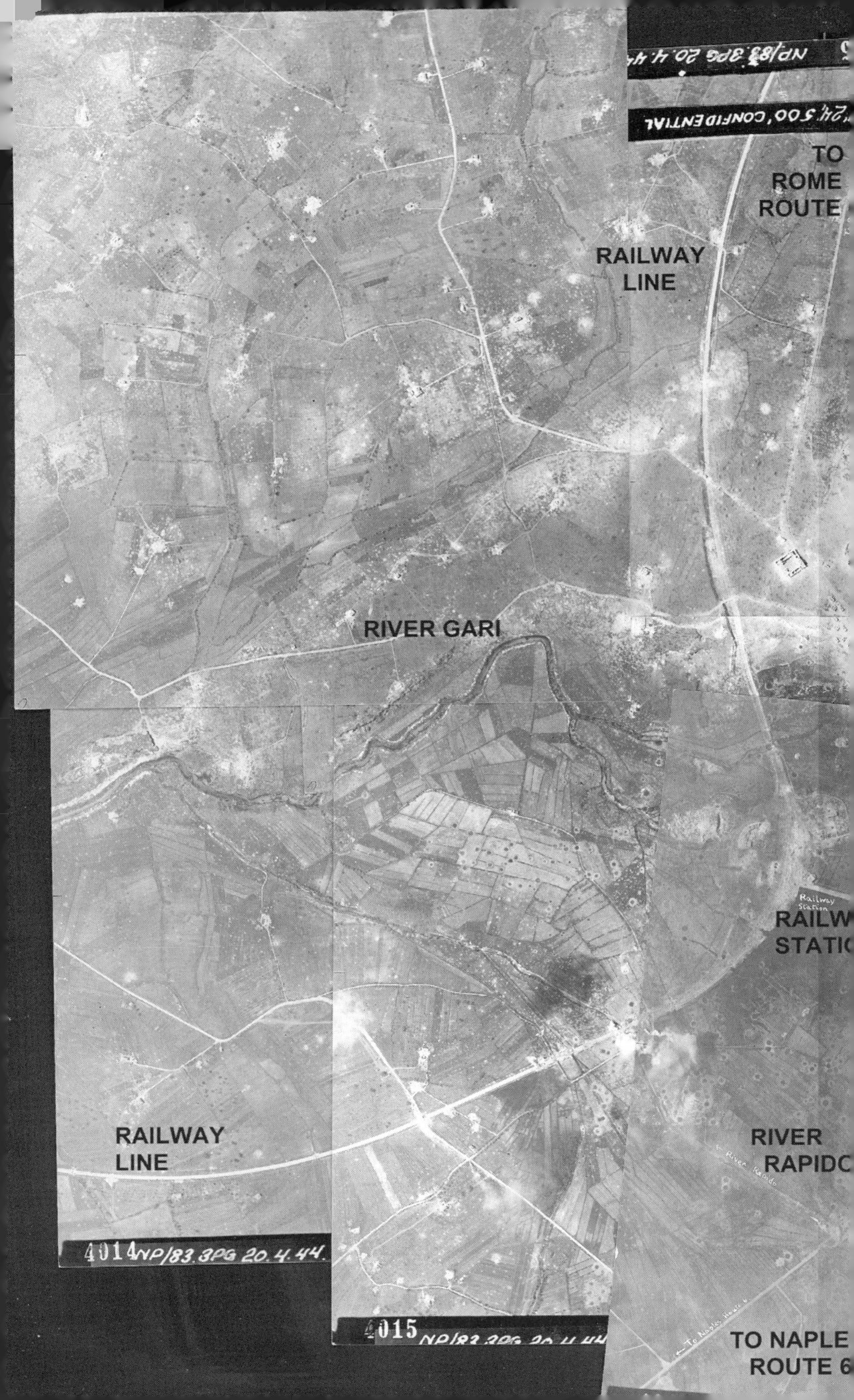
TO
ROME
ROUTE
RAILWAY
LINE
RIVER GARI
Railway
Station
RAILW
STATIO
RAILWAY
LINE
RIVER
RAPIDO
River Rapido
TO NAPLE
ROUTE 6
4014 NP/83.3PG 20.4.44.
4015 NP/83.3PG 20.4.44
NP/83.3PG 20.4.44
24; 500' CONFIDENTIAL

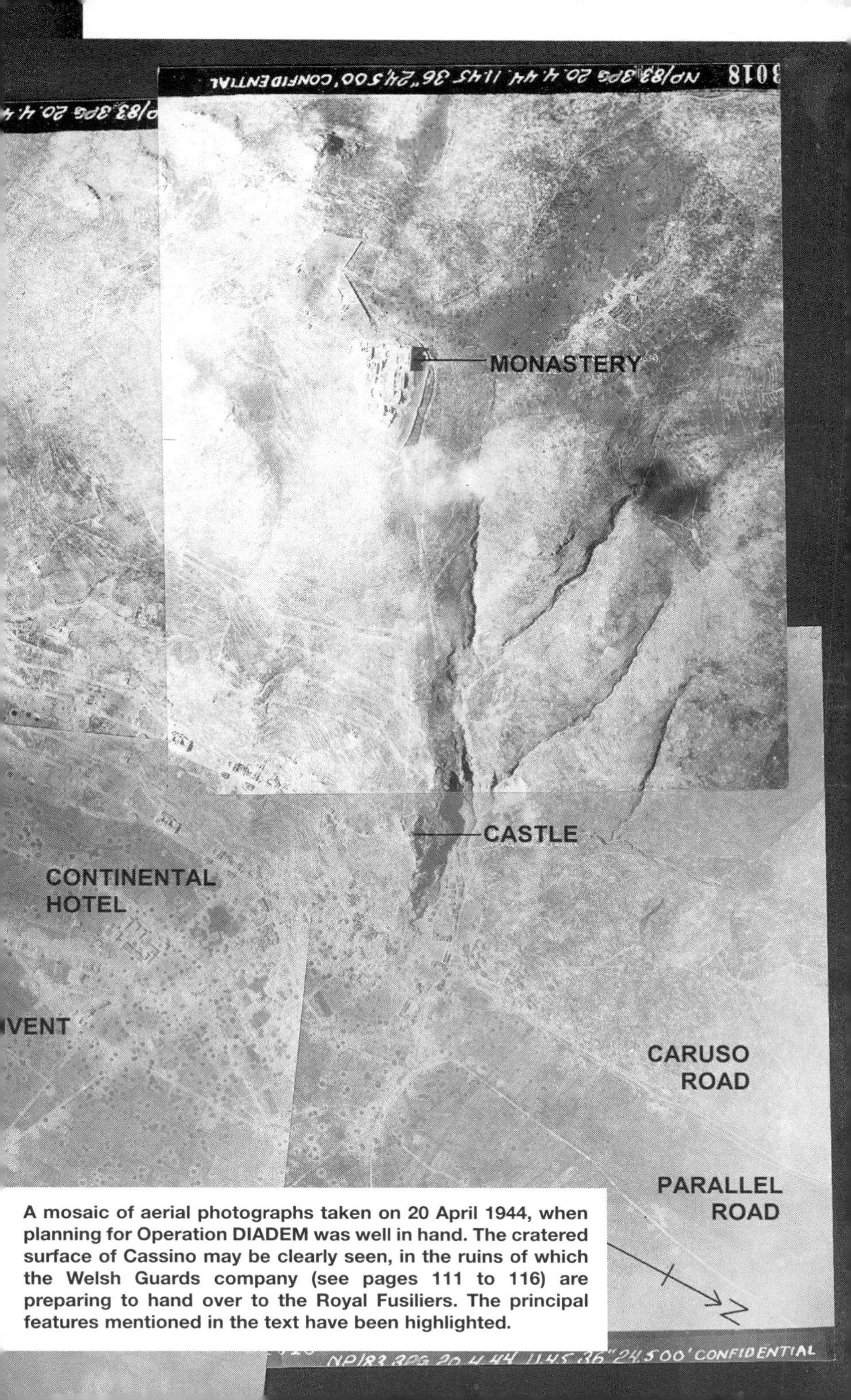

MONASTERY
CASTLE
CONTINENTAL HOTEL
VENT
CARUSO ROAD
PARALLEL ROAD
NP/83 3PG 20.4.44 11.45 36"24.500' CONFIDENTIAL

A mosaic of aerial photographs taken on 20 April 1944, when planning for Operation DIADEM was well in hand. The cratered surface of Cassino may be clearly seen, in the ruins of which the Welsh Guards company (see pages 111 to 116) are preparing to hand over to the Royal Fusiliers. The principal features mentioned in the text have been highlighted.

King George VI visits the scene of the
heavy fighting around Cassino July, 1944.
Right: the column to commemorate the
event at Trocchio. Author

THIS PATH
WALKED ON
TWENTY SEC
DAY OF J
BY HIS MAJ
KING GEORG
ON THE OC
OF HIS VISI

Memorial at Trocchio to the people in the area, both military and civilian, who died
during the war. To its side is a 6-pounder anti-tank gun. Author

Chapter One

TROCCHIO – Stand 1

From the centre of Cassino, take **Route 6, signposted Naples**, under the modern flyover. The road heads towards the village of Cervaro, but **before** reaching it there is a **small crossroads with traffic lights**, on the right-hand corner of which is a slip road. **Turn into this road**, and park when safe, before **walking back** to the crossroads. On the small traffic island between the slip road and the main crossroads is a column bearing the British coat of arms of lion and unicorn, and an inscription recording the visit of King George VI to Cassino on the 22 July 1944. Because of the number of mines still lying in the town ruins at that time, his movements were severely restricted.

Facing towards the town from the crossroads, you are looking down the road leading into Cassino, which had to be travelled by troops and vehicles under the direct gaze of the Germans on the mountain slopes behind. This road was subject to constant fire, observed during the day, and on fixed lines by night, and those who had to travel it did so at top speed. Jeep drivers suffered the extra hazard of not being able to hear the sound of incoming shells over the sound of their revving motors, and of negotiating the badly shot-up road in darkness. This road, and at least one other, was referred to by the troops as the 'Mad Mile'. The name also appears on maps from the New Zealand unit histories, where it is applied to part of the Caruso road running from Caira into Cassino, again in view of the German defenders on the mountain slopes above it. **Return to your car**.

Drive along the road running along the western edge (i.e. the Cassino side) of Mount Trocchio, pausing where possible to view the ground through the trees to your right. There are a couple of places where good panoramas can be gained over the town and the mountains beyond, and it is worth stopping twice to take in the full picture, which cannot all be seen from either of the stops. Some **500 yards** from the crossroads, it is possible to see most of the features shown on the photograph over the page. The eye is particularly drawn to the Monastery, which dominates the valley beneath, and to Point 593, which is marked by the white obelisk of the Polish Memorial. Driving further along the road for **another half-mile** or so, the road crests a small rise, on the other side of which is a fire-break on the hillside to the left. This is a safe **place to park**, and a good view across the valley can be gained from the Cassino side of the road.

Again, the most dominant feature is the Monastery, which from this standpoint obscures Point 593. From the Monastery, Snakeshead

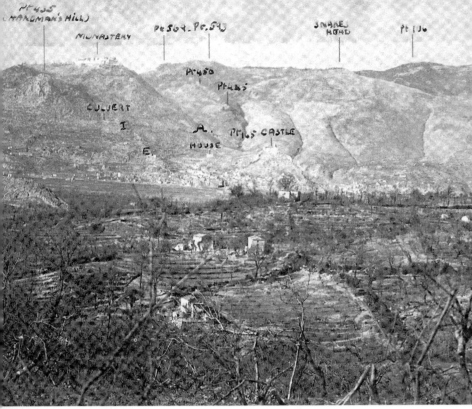

The view from Trocchio. Photograph annotated by CO 9 Gurkha Rifles from an OP. Photograph courtesy the Gurkha Museum

Much of the same view from Trocchio today – but with the post-war reconstruction and vegetation contrasting with the 1944 scenery.

Ridge can be seen extending along the crestline to the right. It was along this crest that firstly the troops of the 34th (US) Infantry Division, then the Sussex Regiment, the Rajputs and the Gurkhas, and finally the Poles attacked in the First, Second, and Fourth Battles of Cassino.

Using the Monastery as the centre of an imaginary clock, the Castle can be clearly seen at four o'clock, and Hangman's Hill is the outcrop of rock immediately below the left-hand end of the Monastery. The road can be seen winding its way up to the top. To the right of the Castle, at the foot of the mountain slopes, lies the quarry. To the right of this again, although not clearly visible, are the Barracks, which were one of the objectives of the Americans during the First Battle.

Firstly the Castle, then the road bend above it, and finally Hangman's Hill were stages in the Allied plan for Third Cassino. You will remember that the town was heavily bombed and was reduced to rubble as a prelude to the ground attack, and that the Germans had cleared the undergrowth and flooded the riverbanks as precautionary measures before the battle. The valley today is therefore much more cluttered by buildings and vegetation than it was in 1944, and some of the key points are now obscured. Two of these are the railway line and the station, which was attacked by the 28 New Zealand (Maori) Battalion during both the Second and Third Battles. Foliage allowing, the station may be made out – indistinctly – as a pale ochre flat-roofed building in the town, immediately beneath the right-hand end of the Monastery, just above the line of the modern road flyover. The railway line itself is mostly out of sight, but curves through the undergrowth from the station, firstly to the right, and then back left again as it moves towards the southern end of Mount Trocchio. It was along the final stretch

New Zealand Artillery OP on Trocchio. New Zealand Electronic Text Centre

of line that the Maoris advanced into the outskirts of Cassino.

During the months of December 1943 until the Cassino Battles were finally over, Trocchio was alive with Allied observation posts. It was the place from which most of the planning and artillery shoots were directed:

It was great fun up on Trocchio except when Jerry lobbed airburst shells just overhead. The 'OP' was a rock sangar on the crest, roofed over with corrugated iron and camouflaged on top with sods. It was equipped with a powerful telescope with which the guns could be directed very accurately on any given spot or house, for instance, or even one particular window in a house. The Kiwis had every inch of Jerry's ground mapped out, all his infantry and guns, the exact location of his horrid Nebelwerfers or 'Moaning Minnies' which scared the life out of everyone as their big clumsy bombs whined through the air. Any suspicious movement or flash of a hostile gun was open to the alert eyes on Trocchio, and bad luck for the German who did not get back under cover smartly. The tanks (though their crews never saw it) completed the ruin of several houses near the river, and helped to spoil the look of Jerry's front-line villages, Sant' Angelo on the opposite riverbank and Pignataro a little farther back; though it was found later that Jerry, in his dugouts under the house floors, was almost immune from any shelling. Farther to the left, in the hills to the south of the Liri valley, the tanks sometimes shot up the village of Sant' Apollinare to oblige the Free French, who were responsible for that part of the front. Some of the 'stonks' consisted of as many as 400 shells. Against the solid stone houses armour-piercing high-explosive shells (APHE for short) were the best, for ordinary high explosive just left slight dents on the walls. But if you wanted to demoralise a gun crew, then high explosive was the thing, preferably airburst.

(18 NZ Battalion and Armoured Regiment History)

Continue along the road until it bends to the left at a small hamlet where the road splits. **The right-hand fork**, the via Callegrande, has a memorial to those of the area, both military and civilian, who died during the war. To its side is a 6-pounder anti-tank gun.

Drive on **southwards taking the road to the left of the fork** and go **across the crossroads**. As you motor towards this point, the rear of Mount Trocchio comes into view on the left, showing the assembly areas for the attacks which took place by the 36th US (Texas) Division on 20 January 1944 and during Operation DIADEM in May of the same year. Both the Texans and the Royal Engineers used this area in preparation for the attempts to bridge the river, towards which you are now moving. **Cross the flyover** on the modern autostrada and **turn right** at the next T-junction towards the village of **Sant' Angelo in Theodice**. Park near the monuments on the **near side** of the bridge.

Chapter Two

THE BRIDGE AT SANT' ANGELO IN THEODICE Stand 2.

There are two monuments before you, one to commemorate the Cassino Battles and to venerate peace; and the other in memory of the 100th Battalion of the US Army, which served with the 34th (US) Infantry Division. This unit was recruited from Hawaiians of Japanese extraction, and fought with distinction in the Italian Campaign. Why the memorial has been placed here, when the battalion fought further to the north, in the mountains, is unclear. Apparently, it was erected by a French author who wrote about the unit.

Monte Cassino is clearly visible to the right, with Monte Trocchio back down the road you have just driven. The route you came was to the south of that followed by 141 Regimental Combat Team (RCT) of the US 36th (Texas) Division as it moved down to the river in its attempt to force a crossing on the night of 20 January 1944. 143 RCT passed to the south. The site of 141 Regiment's attempt on the river is situated near the current flyover to your north, and is now obscured by the trees; the northernmost crossing point for 143 RCT was half a mile downstream from the village, and the southern one about 500 yards further south again.

The attempt to force the river here was part of the operation to cross the Rapido-Gari-Garigliano river system along its length from Cassino down to the sea. As recounted in the earlier overview narrative, the plan was for 46th (British) Division to cross the Garigliano opposite San' Ambroglio on 17 January 1944 and to cover the Americans' left flank when they attacked three days later. The Anzio landing was scheduled for 22 January, by which time the Allies should have been well into the Liri Valley, pushing towards the beachhead. Things do not always go as planned, however. Beset by fog and strong enemy resistance, 46th Division failed to make the crossing and the Texas attack across the Gari River had to proceed without their support.

The Texans faced a number of problems even before this. Major General Fred Walker, the Divisional Commander, had doubts about the operation. A veteran of the 1918 Battle of the Marne, where he had been

Major General Fred Walker, GOC 36th (Texas) Division
Associazone Battaglia di Cassino

awarded the Distinguished Service Cross for his part in repelling a strong German attack across the river which gave the battle its name, he had few illusions about the difficulties of his mission, knowing all too well the advantages which lay with the defender of a river crossing. At his level of command he was unaware of the wider strategic picture and could not see the importance of the operation; rather he was inclined to see it as not being worth the cost in lives which would inevitably follow. Without support on his left flank he would have preferred to delay or to cancel; he confided in his diary that he was

Men of 36th (Texas) Division watching artillery fire on the Gustav Line. Monte Cairo in the background, Monte Cassino and the Monastery can be seen below it. Associazone Battaglia di Cassino

View today from the bridge at Sant' Angelo, with key features annotated on Monte Cassino. Author

American soldiers moving smoke canisters forward for the attack.
Associazone Battaglia di Cassino

prepared for defeat and that the mission should not have been contemplated if his flanks were exposed. His relationship with both Clark and Major General Geoffrey Keyes, his Corps Commander, was not of the closest and there was a reluctance to appear to be too negative about the plan, which held him back from expressing his reservations strongly. It is fair to say that he was not committed to the operation and remained unconvinced of its ability to succeed. Such doubts did not augur well for his drive and leadership, or for the outcome of the battle.

Nevertheless, planning proceeded. The initial crossing was to be made by infantry in assault boats, who would establish a bridgehead on the far bank before the engineers constructed footbridges to allow more troops to cross. Finally, a Bailey Bridge would be erected so that armour might push on through to the Liri Valley, and to facilitate the exploitation of the bridgehead. While this may have sounded practicable from a distance, the state of the ground and the river itself conspired to throw the plans into disarray, apart from any efforts of the Germans, who had wired and mined the approaches and had ranged in artillery targets observed from the surrounding heights. The river banks were three feet above the swiftly-flowing water, itself nine feet deep and forty to fifty feet wide. The fact that canoeists use the river beneath the bridge today – and in the summer - as a slalom course, gives a small indication of its condition in the winter months of 1944, when the weather was at its worst. Engineers who carried out reconnaissance missions to sweep for mines and to identify crossing points were hampered by German fire and by fighting patrols, which were believed to have re-laid mines in the cleared lanes.

At a practical level, there was a shortage of suitable boats and bridging equipment. Twelve DUKWs, which should have been available, had been lost during training sessions for the Anzio landings – but their worth was in any respect questionable because of the height of the river banks which would have made their passage in and out of the water extremely difficult, if not impossible. The standard engineer footbridge was unavailable, and plans were set in place for inflatable reconnaissance boats, plywood assault boats, and make-shift footbridges constructed from pneumatic floats and Bailey bridge catwalks to be brought forward. Although there was no rain in the ten days before the attack, the ground in the river valley was still waterlogged and impassible to vehicles. The material was therefore gathered in two dumps near the base of Trocchio, some miles from the crossing points, and would have to be carried to the river bank by the infantry and assembled under engineer direction. This presented another problem, for although engineers had practiced their role with the infantry before the operation, they had done so on the Volturno River in relatively calm conditions which were not to be experienced on the Gari. To compound the difficulty, 142 and 143 RCTs had taken part in the training, but Walker later replaced 142 RCT with 141 RCT as one of the units to carry out the attack, to even out the time spent in combat by each of his regiments. This was to contribute to a lack of

Plywood assault boats, looking ominously like coffins, lined up ready for the Americans to cross under fire.

cooperation between the infantry and the engineers, a factor which was to bedevil the operation as they failed to understand their roles or to work effectively together. An engineer complaint was that the infantry did not consult them on the operation, and then blamed them for failure when it went awry.

141 RCT

Just upstream from Sant' Angelo 141 RCT planned to cross in assault boats in line abreast with the three companies of one battalion (the First, or 1/141), to establish a bridgehead about three-quarters of a mile deep. A second battalion would follow in boats and across four footbridges to be constructed by the engineers. This was to take place in the area of the modern autostrada flyover to the north, now covered by trees. On the late afternoon of 20 January 1944 the troops left their assembly areas to collect their boats from the dumps. Several had been destroyed or damaged by German artillery fire, but selecting the usable ones from the debris, the battalion worked its way forward to the river bank at about 1900 hours, in the thick fog that had descended at nightfall. Thirty minutes later, sixteen battalions of American artillery with additional support from 4.2-inch mortars began to lay down a barrage on the opposite bank, programmed to creep forward in advance of the infantry. This brought swift retaliation from the Germans, whose shells brought havoc to the Americans. One company lost thirty men, and some of those who scattered for cover strayed into the minefields, the marker-tape for which had been blasted out of position or buried in the mud. At least twenty-five per cent of the boats and footbridges were lost, and men became separated from their guides. By the time they arrived at the river bank these losses in

Men from 36th (Texas) Division crossing under fire. Associazone Battaglia di Cassino

equipment had doubled. Boats, riddled with holes, sank; others drifted away and some overturned as the inexpert crews attempted to paddle across the swiftly-flowing river. By 2100 hours a handful of men were across, but were forced to dig in and defend themselves against German resistance.

With no complete footbridge surviving the journey to the river, the engineers had to cannibalise what parts they could find. At 0400 hours on 21 January a single span was completed, and although it was damaged by shellfire an hour later it provided an unsteady but workable passage. Using the bridge and the few remaining boats, about half of 1/141 crossed by 0630 hours. There they remained, with contact lost once the radios became inoperable and the field telephone wires had been broken by artillery fire. With daylight approaching and no means of reinforcing the men on the far bank in the face of more accurately targeted German fire, the two supporting battalions of 141 RCT were ordered back into cover by Brigadier General Wilbur, the Assistant Divisional Commander. At about the same time, Lieutenant Colonel Wyatt, the regimental commander, ordered the troops back from the far bank. Few of them were able to make the journey. The remainder dug in, without means of communication to their rear or the possibility of reinforcement, and

Texans on the river in daylight.
Associazone Battaglia di Cassino

awaited the inevitable German counterattack. Those on the eastern banks could only follow events by the sounds of battle which came from across the water.

At 2100 hours on 21 January, 141 RCT attacked again. Sixty men from Company F of 2/141, in whatever undamaged boats they could find, paddled across the river. They found no survivors of the company from the First Battalion, which had crossed during the previous night. It took them five hours to clear the area of Germans and for two improvised footbridges to be pushed over the river, across which were fed a whole battalion. With the aid of a third bridge, the rifle companies of a second battalion (3/141) made the passage. By dawn, six rifle companies and some heavy weapons sections were on the western side. They advanced about 100 yards before digging in under enemy fire.

Behind them the engineers were struggling through the sodden ground to bring forward a Bailey Bridge. By 0945 hours, the attempt was temporarily suspended and then abandoned. Troops on the far side of the river were unable to advance, and those on the near bank could not assist them, and inertia set in. By early afternoon the balance swung against the Americans. To the south, 143 RCT had withdrawn to the eastern bank, freeing-up Germans from their crossing point to concentrate on the 141 bridgehead. Communications were cut, all of the boats and bridges were destroyed, and by the evening only one officer remained alive and unwounded. Little could be done to assist the trapped men, and all American troops on the far bank were dead or captured, apart from about forty who swam back during the evening. By 2000 hours firing on the western side of the river had ceased.

143 RCT

Below the village 143 RCT had selected two crossing sites. At the first, half a mile south of Sant' Angelo, a battalion would cross in boats with the three companies in column, one after the other. Five hundred yards further south a second battalion would cross in the same fashion. Once the leading companies were established on the far bank, the engineers would start building two footbridges at each site, across which the following companies would advance.

Here the advance units reached their crossing points with little difficulty, and a platoon crossed the Gari at 2000 hours. The boats, empty but for their engineer crews, came under artillery fire as they returned; all of them were sunk and heavy casualties were inflicted on both banks. A footbridge pushed across the river twenty minutes later was destroyed, and it was impossible to carry out immediate repairs under the intensified shelling. By 2145 hours, however, extra boats were brought to the bank, and two more footbridges were thrown across despite the shelling. The remaining men of the first company, numbers depleted by casualties, made the journey to the far side. These were reinforced by 0500 hours the following day, after the regimental commander, Colonel Martin, fetched five more boats with the assistance of engineers whom he had ordered out of their foxholes. A battalion (1/143) was now across, but artillery fire then destroyed one bridge and so damaged the other that it could be used by only one man at a time. Two hours later, the troops on the far bank were pushed into a pocket with their backs to the river.

Major Frazior, the batalion commander, saw no prospect of establishing a firm foothold on the western side of the river. Nor could he see a way of getting into Sant' Angelo. He therefore requested permission to pull his men back, a request that was passed to Walker, who refused it, telling them to stay where they were and to await reinforcements. However, by the time the messages had taken to pass back and forth, Frazior had taken the decision to order the withdrawal while his men were still able to make the crossing back to a more friendly shore. Under fire from enemy artillery, mortars and tanks, those who were able to do so were back by 1000 hours.

At the other 143 RCT crossing site the engineers leading the boat-

Retiring from the attempt on the Rapido. Wounded GIs being evacuated.
Associazone Battaglia di Cassino

carrying parties lost their way in the darkness and fog and walked into a minefield, where men and boats suffered heavy losses. Disorganised and huddled near the river, the survivors made little effort to cross. Colonel Martin relieved the battalion commander, Major Ressijac, whom he had lost confidence in, but even with a fresh leader no move forward was made. Shortly before daybreak the assault companies pulled back to their original positions.

Using the same sites as previously, 3/143 RCT got three rifle companies and the heavy weapons company (less the mortar sections) over the upper crossing on 21 January 1944. Starting at 1600 hours under cover of smoke, they crossed in boats and by midnight the engineers had a footbridge erected which helped the passage of the rest of the battalion, including the headquarters element. Two further companies from the Second Battalion followed. They got no further than 500 yards from the river when they ran into strong resistance and had to dig in. Without armoured support, they could not proceed, but armour required a Bailey Bridge to cross. Under fire, the engineers could not even begin to build one, not least because by the time the components had been brought forward, dawn was about to break and they would have been naked to view from the German-occupied mountains.

At the second site, downriver, two rifle companies of 1/143 RCT had crossed by 1830 hours. Heavy German shelling stopped them being reinforced for another four hours, when part of a third company joined them and a footbridge was completed. The battalion commander, Major Frazior, was wounded when he went forward to find out why the advance had come to a standstill no more than 200 yards from the bank. By 0500 hours all three company commanders had been wounded and all the boats and the footbridge destroyed, a depressingly familiar scenario. Despite managing to erect two more footbridges (which became routes for retreating and wounded soldiers) the numbers of Americans on the far bank steadily decreased until no more than 250 remained at daybreak. With no hope of supporting them with

US 36th 'Texas' Infantry Division. 'T' for Texas on an indian arrowhead.

armour, they were withdrawn at noon. A few isolated groups were left, cut off.

36th (Texas) Division suffered 1,681 casualties during the two-day battle. Additional numbers were suffered by the supporting arms – the engineers, artillery, Quartermaster Corps, and so on, who were attached to the division for the operation. For the time being, those units which had been involved in the action ceased to be an effective

Graves of the 36th (Texas) Division near Monte Trocchio in 1945. Some of these bodies were later repatriated to the United States, others moved to the American War Cemetery at Nettunio. Associazone Battaglia di Cassino

fighting force. On the German side, the defending troops from *15 Panzer Grenadier Division* had negligible losses, and their reports of the battle made little of it, stating only that they had 'prevented enemy troops from crossing'. It was not until later that von Senger realized that the attacks were part of a larger Fifth Army offensive which included the Anzio landings.

To add insult to injury, the Germans released a captured carrier pigeon, to which they had attached a message which read:

> *Herewith a messenger pigeon is returned. We have enough to eat and what's more, we look forward with pleasure to your next attempt.*

The decision to proceed with the attack, which led to such high casualties, naturally rankled with the Texans. After the war they demanded, and got, a Congressional Enquiry into the affair. General Clark claimed that the attack had tied down German units along the Gustav Line and drawn divisions from the Anzio area, a claim disputed by General Walker, who maintained that this move was in response to the British attack on the Garigliano, which is indeed where they were sent. Furthermore, they were withdrawn back to Anzio on 22 January 1944, as were an infantry regiment and some artillery units.

Clark was vindicated by the enquiry, but the argument still continues.

Drive **across the bridge** and **turn right** into the town centre. Stop at the small square on the right.

Chapter Three

THE TOWN CENTRE, SANT' ANGELO IN THEODICE Stand 3.

From the car park there is a good view back across the river towards Trocchio and the bridge, and the clear fields of fire that the Germans had against the Allied attackers, first the Americans in January and then the 8th Indian and 78th British Divisions in May, are apparent. Allied lines of advance from the southern (right-hand from here) shoulder of Trocchio are clearly in sight, and in 1944 the undergrowth had been removed and the ground strewn with wire and mines. In the winter months much of the ground was sodden and difficult to cross.

In the small square is a monument to 36th (Texas) Division, bearing its insignia of an Indian Arrowhead.

Memorial to the 36th (Texas) Division.
Author

During the final battle for Cassino, the Allies planned to build seven Bailey Bridges across the Gari and Garigliano Rivers. XIII Corps was to force a passage with 4th Division on the right and 8th (Indian) Division left. Sant' Angelo was in 8th (Indian) Division's sector, and its river crossing points – from north to south – were code-named CARDIFF (Class 30, capable of bearing tanks), LONDON (Class 40), OXFORD (Class 30), and PLYMOUTH (Class 30). Ferries were also to be constructed.

At 2300 hours on the night of 11 May, the attack opened all along the front with an artillery barrage by some 900 guns, coordinated by the time-pips signal from the BBC. Instead of withdrawing, the

77

Infantry picking their way through the ruins of Sant' Angelo.

Sherman tanks, Bren gun carriers and anti-tank guns in action near a dried-out river bed.

Germans moved troops down to the river bank and thickened the evening mist with smoke until visibility was almost completely lost, even obscuring the tracer from Bofors guns with which the Indians were indicating the line of advance. Although the approaches to the river presented fewer difficulties than the Americans had faced earlier in the year, being much drier in the spring weather, the Gari itself presented a formidable obstacle. Flowing more swiftly than the rivers on which they had practiced the crews of the assault boats found themselves in difficulties and many were swept downstream.

Sant' Angelo itself was the target of 17 (Indian) Infantry Brigade, and the intention was to pinch the village (or the remnants of it – by this stage in the battles it was in ruins) out from the south by the 1/12 Frontier Force Regiment and by 1 Royal Fusiliers from the north. Launching their assault boats at 2345 hours, both battalions crossed the river without major difficulty, but the Fusiliers found themselves hemmed in between the village and a defensive position known as the 'Platform' knoll to the north. Until these were cleared no further advance was possible. The Frontiersmen reached the embankment on the road running behind the village and parallel to the river, but their attack was held up by mines and wire, the radios failed, and in the thick fog of German smoke visual methods of communication were useless. Above the noise of battle came the Mussulman war cry 'Maro nari haidriya Ali!' which gave the battalion commander his men's positions and enabled him to bring some degree of order to events. The Frontiersmen waited until dawn before advancing further, and despite taking casualties from machineguns in Sant' Angelo succeeded in establishing a firm foothold on the approaches to the village.

1/5 Gurkha Rifles, in support, lost twelve of the sixteen boats with which they were to cross the Gari, and had to use the remaining craft on fixed ropes to ferry their men across, a process which took five hours. Two companies were sent forward to attack Sant' Angelo, but became entangled with the Frontiersmen in the fog. It was 1700 hours by the time they had redeployed, and the attack commenced with troops of Canadian tanks from 11 (Ontario) Armoured Regiment in support. One company of Gurkhas cleared a machinegun nest in a house on the flank, the other destroyed seven machinegun posts and their crews with a rush, but the tanks became bogged down before they could get into the fight. Again the Gurkhas had to dig in, postponing the attack until the next day. The village finally fell on the 13 May 1944. The Frontiersmen and Gurkhas were pulled back to allow seven field regiments to bombard the village in a five-minute shoot, then two companies of Gurkhas dashed forward supported by tank fire, gaining the outskirts within fifteen minutes. In an hour's fighting, with no quarter asked or given, Sant' Angelo was taken. A number of fanatical Germans had to be killed in the cellars, and those few who fled were cut down by tanks which had been positioned to stop their escape. The capture of this keystone in the Gari defence cost 1/5 Gurkhas ten officers and 119 men.

Having observed the fall of Sant' Angelo the Germans on 'Platform' knoll surrendered, leaving 1 Royal Fusiliers free to advance, and to the south of the village the 1/12 Frontier Force Regiment was now able to

Sepoy Kamal Ram, VC, 3/8 Punjab Regiment.
Associazone Battaglia di Cassino

move up the entrance to the Liri valley.

19 Indian Infantry Brigade crossed the Gari to the south of 17 Brigade. The right-hand battalion, the 3/8 Punjabis, sustained many casualties from German defensive fire as it moved up to the river. A number of assault boats were carried away in the current, forcing the battalion to cross using only one boat and two rafts, a procedure which was extremely time-consuming and left it well behind its artillery programme. When finally in place for its attack on the German side of the river, it was 0530 hours and dawn was breaking. Fortunately, the German-laid smoke was thick enough to conceal the Punjabis, but the line of their advance was betrayed by the exploding mines into which they moved. Company after company was pinned down by machinegun fire, with heavy casualties. Sepoy Kamal Ram, aged nineteen, responded to his company commander's call for a volunteer to deal with a machinegun on the right flank. He crawled through the wire and attacked the crew single-handed, shooting the gunner and bayoneting the loader, before killing a German officer who came at him with a pistol from a slit trench. He then sniped the gunner of a second nest and bombed the rest of the team into surrendering, before dealing with a third position – this time accompanied by a havildar – in a similar manner. Later in the day he accounted for a fourth machinegun nest. For his bravery, Kamal Ram was awarded the Victoria Cross.

6/13 Frontier Force and tanks of 14 (Calgary) Armoured Regiment, working in close cooperation, cleared the high ground towards Panaccioni, destroying hidden German tanks and self-propelled guns as they advanced. Panaccioni fell at 1400 hours on 13 May 1944.

Chapter Four

AMAZON BRIDGE Stand 4.

Drive through Sant' Angelo village and **turn right** on the road towards Cassino. Having passed under the flyover, and as you approach the first buildings on the outskirts of Cassino, you will cross a **small bridge** over a rivulet, parallel to which, on the right hand side, is a slip road signposted **Via S. Brigada**. Turn **right** down this road. Keep bearing right until you pass a farmhouse on the right. Shortly after the farm is a dirt track to the left, just before a large cattle shed. **Parking** should be done with care because of the narrowness of the paved road, which is often used by agricultural vehicles, but weather and mud conditions may make a decision to **park just off the paved road** more sensible than attempting to get closer to the river by using the track. Walk down the track, which bears to the left and follows the river bank until you come to a sharp bend in the River Gari. You are now in the area attacked by 4th Division, which advanced with 10 Brigade on the right, 28 Brigade to its left, and 12 Brigade in support. On the bend in the river, immediately to the right of where you are standing, is the site of AMAZON Bridge.

The River Gari, site of Amazon Bridge today, with undergrowth masking the appraoches. Author

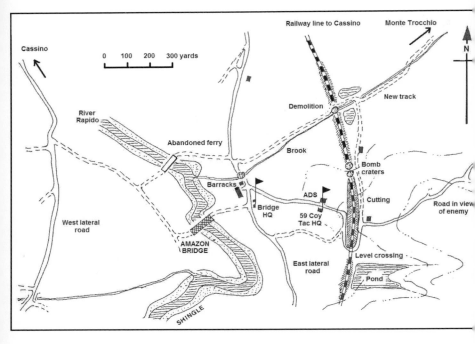

From north to south 4th Division's bridge points were code-named AMAZON (Class 40), BLACKWATER (Class 9, capable of bearing trucks, as a return route for vehicles moving back from the bridgeheads), and CONGO (Class 40), These were to be built by 7, 59 and 225 Field Companies, Royal Engineers, immediately after the infantry had crossed the river in assault boats.

Advancing into this dense fog of mist and German smoke carrying their assault boats, the 4th Division infantry from 10 and 28 Brigades, north and south respectively, soon became disoriented, many getting lost and going around in circles while under machinegun and mortar fire. Although the 10 Brigade battalions got most of their men across the river, 28's were less successful. Arriving behind schedule, 2 King's Regiment were too late to take advantage of the artillery barrage and by the time they crossed the river German fire was dropping heavily on them. Determined resistance met the elements of the three companies that made it through the shell and machinegun fire. 2 Somerset Light Infantry, which should have passed through the King's, ran into stragglers from that battalion and two companies became disorganised and withdrew.

In the chaos it proved impossible for the sappers to move their equipment forward, and when dawn broke they came under heavy fire from Minenwerfers directed from Monte Cassino. The following night all three of 4th Division's Field Companies were employed in an attempt to throw a single Bailey across the river. The site selected for this concentrated effort was 'AMAZON', and each company was to work in turn on the bridge, being relieved by the next when it became exhausted. Shortly after 1700 hours 225 Field Company commenced work, with 7 and 59 Field Companies waiting to follow when required. As construction was under way, the Germans fired Very lights behind the building site which silhouetted the sappers and made them easy targets for enemy snipers. Under shell, mortar, sniper and Spandau fire, which disabled the blade elevating gear on a bulldozer and wounded the OC 7 Company, the work went on. A call for counter battery fire brought down the combined efforts of five Medium and two Field Regiments onto the German gunners, which stopped their activities for some time. Sergeant Parry of 59 Field Company crossed the river on the nose of the bridge as it was pushed across, and dealt with two Spandaus which had been causing casualties. He was awarded the Military Medal for his courage. The bridge was completed by 0400 hours, but eighty-three sappers were lost from 7 and 225 Field Companies.

The crossing by 10 and 28 Infantry Brigades had not proceeded well, and with both now pinned down, the Divisional Commander committed his remaining brigade, the 12th. At 2200 hours on 12 May, his orders were passed to the commanding officers. 6 Black Watch would cross AMAZON, followed by 2 Royal Fusiliers, which would position itself on the right before moving forward, each battalion supported by a squadron of tanks from the Lothian and Border Horse.

German nebelwerfer – the 'Moaning Minnie' – in the Liri Valley
Associazone Battaglia di Cassino

Delayed by the problems in completing the bridge, the timetable was further thrown back by having to cross the Pioppeto River, which lay beyond the Gari. The armoured fighting vehicle carrying the scissors bridge – which was the only practicable solution to getting tanks over this obstacle – was hit while crossing the Gari, and further delay ensued while it was cleared. The infantry waiting to follow came under fire, and took cover until the bridge was cleared at 0700 hours on 13 May, when they were able to cross. A hurried attack was planned: the Black Watch would move to the left, the Fusiliers to the right, with groups of farm buildings some 1,000 yards ahead as the objectives, beyond the road which runs behind you and parallel to the river. Dashing forward over the bridge approaches, the troops had to pass ground littered with the bodies of sappers and of soldiers from 10 Brigade who had made the boat crossing.

Once on the west bank, and having dealt with small groups of German machine-gunners and snipers, the two battalions were packed

Major Michael Gibson-Horrocks, 2nd Battalion Royal Fusiliers.

into an area a few hundred yards square, immediately around the bridgehead – the area between where you now stand and the road running parallel to the river. Here they came under artillery and mortar fire which took a heavy toll. The Royal Fusiliers suffered – Major Michael Gibson-Horrocks, commanding Y Company, was wounded during the reconnaissance; the three platoon commanders and all but eighteen men of the original 100 from Z Company were casualties, as was the company commander. By the end of the day each company was down to one officer and thirty men. They had, however, reached their objectives. The bridgehead had expanded from fifty to 1,000 yards deep, and supporting units were now able to move forward. Shermans from the Lothians joined them, but – following the doctrine of the time – withdrew just before dark as they were considered too vulnerable. This was small comfort for the infantry, but they were back the following day to support 2 Bedfordshire and Hertfordshire Regiment when they advanced through the position in an unsuccessful attempt to cut Route 6.

Reorganised into two companies, 'WX' and 'YZ', the Royal Fusiliers held onto their positions in the bridgehead for two days, through

Shermans supporting a bridgehead across a river in Italy.

which 78th Division passed, advancing parallel to Route 6. The ground over which the Division moved may be more clearly seen from the heights of the Monte Cairo massif, from some of the following Stands. Detailed tracing of the route it took is not so easy, as the valley has been developed with the building of the autostrada and industrial parks.

With the Poles fighting desperately to take the mountain slopes, on 17 May the Fusiliers were ordered to mount another attack to assist in cutting Route 6 and so seal the exit from Cassino town. They moved out but faced no resistance in the mile they had to cover to reach the road. The Germans seemed disorganised and unaware of the situation, and a number of their vehicles drove unsuspectingly into the Fusiliers' positions. The situation could best be described as being fluid, and it was not only the enemy that was confused: a truck carrying mail and a NAAFI van attempted to move towards Rome until halted by bursts of Spandau fire. The mail truck turned tail and headed back eastwards at speed, but the NAAFI driver was persuaded to provide the Fusiliers with tea and wads before withdrawing. He requested, and got, a note stating that 'NAAFI Van *No Orchids for Miss Blandish* had this day served the foremost troops in the British Army. Signed, OC Z Company 2nd Royal Fusiliers'.

German prisoners after the battle.
Associazone Battaglia di Cassino

At first light on 18 May Major Ian Thomas, OC 'WX' Company, and his batman climbed up Monte Cassino. On their way to the summit, a group of some twenty Germans hidden in a cave surrendered to the pair, waving a tablecloth. Arriving at the Monastery at the same time as the Poles, Thomas collected a Polish officer's signature on the fly leaf of his pocket bible before returning to his battalion. The tablecloth is now in the Royal Fusiliers' Museum in the Tower of London.

On 21 May, Lieutenant Colonel Adrian Evans, the Fusiliers' CO, and the Padre, Paul Wansey, came under shellfire when they were assisting the wounded. The Padre, a veteran of France and Tunisia, took cover. The CO elected to remain upright, as he had consistently done on previous occasions, and was killed. The battalion was now withdrawn for a fortnight's rest and reorganisation.

Leave the riverbank and drive back to the Sant' Angelo- Cassino road. **Turn right** and continue to the **Commonwealth War Graves Commission Cemetery**.

Chapter Five

CASSINO COMMONWEALTH WAR GRAVES COMMISSION CEMETERY Stand 5.

Further along the road towards Cassino lies the Commonwealth War Graves Commission Cemetery.

4,266 British and Commonwealth servicemen are buried here, 284 unknown, and over 4,000 of those of no known grave are commemorated on the memorial plaques which stand imposingly along the sides of the central water feature in front of the Cross of Remembrance. Most of the buried died in the fighting here in 1944. The cemetery should be visited for several reasons, the most important of which, of course, is to remember those who sacrificed so much. It is also worth spending time noting the nationalities represented here – the point has already been made that this conflict illustrates the point that it was a world war. Americans who died here were buried at Nettuno, south of Anzio; and there are French, German, Italian and Polish War Cemeteries nearby.

Another reason to dwell amongst the graves is to note the numerous regiments which are represented here, but which no longer form part

View of Monte Cassino from the Cemetery. Hangman's Hill is the rocky outcrop immediately beneath the Monastery. Cassino town is to the right of the photograph. Route 6 runs along the foot of the slopes into the Liri Valley to the left. Author

of the British Army line of battle. Here will be found regiments from the United Kingdom which have lost their titles and independent existence, having long since been more recent casualties of defence cuts and restructuring and amalgamations under new titles and cap-badges, but also those which disappeared with Britain's retreat from Empire – the old Indian Army predominantly, but also other units that no longer exist, such as the Cyprus Regiment. There are also long-lost ranks and appointments, which appear strange to those only acquainted with the modern army. To select but a few of these to illustrate the point, among the graves are those of Sweeper Lachhu, of the Royal Indian Army Service Corps (aged eighteen) and Ambulance Sepoy Thamatu John of the Indian Army Medical Corps lying side by side; in the row behind is Water Carrier Gul Zaman of the Indian General Service Corps. And row upon row of British, Canadian, New Zealand, and other Commonwealth servicemen.

The Cemetery Grounds also give a good viewpoint of the Monastery and Monte Cassino from the entrance to the Liri valley. Hangman's Hill and Point 593 are clearly visible, and from the steps at the front of the Cemetery Monte Trocchio can be seen across the valley to the east.

In the shelter hut on the north side of the graves is a replica of the 9 Gurkha memorial which was placed on Hangman's Hill after the battle, but which is no longer there.

Drive down the road and into **Cassino** town, turning right at the T-junction and **park near the Railway Station**.

Graves of soldiers from by-gone regiments in the Cassino Cemetery. Author

Chapter Six

CASSINO Stand 6.

The town of Cassino was destroyed during the fighting, primarily during the bombing on 15 March 1944, but also because of the artillery fire with which both sides saturated the town. Despite generally keeping to the main pre-war street layout, little of the town would today be recognisable to those who fought here. Post-war buildings, erected as soon as possible after the conflict, replace those that stood here at the end of 1943. Some of these apparently incorporate the remains of German tanks in their foundations, the builders not having the necessary equipment to remove them before construction started. A pre-war edition of Baedike contained the comment that the town of Cassino was of little interest, and that the main attraction in the region was the Monastery itself. The visitor may agree that some things have not changed, despite – or perhaps because of – the re-building. The

Aerial view of Cassino taken in November 1943, Showing Castle Hill in the background. New Zealand Electronic Text Centre

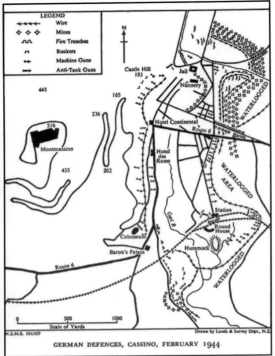

GERMAN DEFENCES, CASSINO, FEBRUARY 1944

German defences Cassino.
New Zealand Electronic Text Centre

town has grown to at least double its pre-war size and now occupies the land all the way east to the River Rapido, as may be seen by comparing the maps of 1944 and today.

One thing has not changed, however, and that is the dominance of Monte Cassino and Rocca Janula (the Castle) over the town. Through the gaps between the modern buildings these features stare down, and provide useful reference points when the visitor sometimes gets disoriented in the streets which today present a confusing similarity to the stranger. The psychological impact of these heights on those fighting in the streets below, is driven home again.

There are a few points of interest remaining in the town. Firstly, the Railway Station itself was rebuilt on its original site, and the railway track follows its former course. On the platform is a memorial to 28 NZ (Maori) Battalion, which advanced thus far during the Second Battle, having come down the railway line from the east. Near the original station was the lower terminus of the pre-war cable-car to the Monastery, an upper gantry of which stood on Hangman's Hill and which led the Allies to give the feature its macabre name. The cable system became inoperative in 1943, when a German aircraft crashed into it.

Route 6 also follows its original course through the town, although

Memorial to the 28th New Zealand (Maori) Battalion on the railway station platform. Author

A British Tommy picks his way through the ruins.

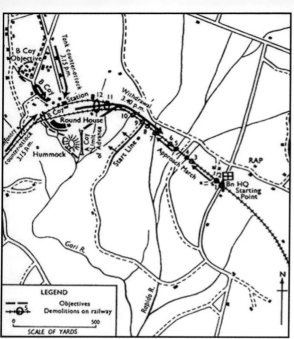

The attack on the railway station.
New Zealand Electronic Text Centre

today part of it is a one-way street, the Repubblica. At the westernmost end of this street, where it meets the road running along the base of the mountain slopes, was situated the Hotel Continental. The Hotel des Roses was to its south, in the angle between the road along the foot of the mountains, and that leading up to the Monastery. Both of these buildings were turned into strongpoints by the Germans, and there are caves in the rockface behind them, visible between the modern buildings, in which German troops sought shelter. The Virgilio d'Annunzio and Dante Roads, which form the 'X'-shaped intersection north of the station, also follow their original layouts.

A cave in the riocks behind modern buildings in Cassino. In 1944, German defenders of the Continental Hotel sheltered here. Author

Before the war, Cassino was a small town, comprising older, more crowded streets, gardens and squares in the north, where it stretched along the two roads, Caruso Road running to Caira and the Parallel Road to Sant' Elia. Branching eastwards and then curving to the northeast was the Pasquale Road.

Outside the town along the western, Caira, road were Italian Army Barracks. The southern end of Cassino was more open and spacious, following more recent planning policies during the Mussolini regime. Here was the railway station with its roundhouse, and the cable car terminus.

Fighting for, and in, the town was heavy. Although the American main effort had largely by-passed it during the First Battle, pushing into the mountains to the north of its outskirts, they had made incursions into its outer limits down the Caruso Road, and the town itself was a major Allied objective during the Second and Third Battles.

The Second Battle

Having relieved 34th (US) Division in the Cassino area after its unsuccessful attacks on 11 February 1944, the New Zealand Corps prepared to take up the cudgels. 4th Indian Division would follow the lines of attack that the Americans had taken along Snakeshead Ridge to the Monastery via Point 593; 2nd New Zealand Division would operate in the valley, taking the southern end of the town of Cassino and opening the way for armour to drive into the Liri valley. During the handover period a patrol from 28 NZ (Maori) Battalion with a sapper officer had, on the night of 8 February, investigated the railway line which ran on an embankment into the town. Apart from the ruined railway bridge, there were a total of twelve demolitions along the track which would need bulldozing, bridging or culverts building before tanks could cross them.

During the night of 17/18 February 1944, A and B Companies of the Maori Battalion pushed along the left side of the railway embankment and into the outskirts of Cassino. The ground they crossed was marshy and under water, and unsuitable for digging in support weapons. They advanced down this narrow front with the intention of taking the railway station and the 'Hummocks', a feature which is on the site of the present camping ground south of it. Sappers would follow and fill or bridge the gaps in the embankment and the waterways, which would allow the Sherman tanks of 19 Armoured Regiment to break through to the Liri valley to their left. As the history of the 2nd New Zealand Divisional Artillery puts it, 'To say the plan was curious would be putting it mildly'. The artillery could not support such an attack effectively, 25-pounders being virtually useless against the town

The Monastery and Castle Hill under artillery fire. The houses of the town were reduced to rubble.

A New Zealand infantryman operating a Thompson sub-machine gun at Cassino.

buildings, and not enough medium and heavy guns available to make a difference.

The infantry fought their way into the Station yard and had dug in by midnight, having lost nearly a third of their men as casualties. The sappers, however, found their task more difficult, and when the moon rose at 0300 hours they were brought under observed fire by German mortars and machineguns. Delayed by difficulties in clearing the mines – the mine-detectors had to contend with the iron railway tracks which still lay along the embankment – and faced with a twenty-foot wide creek which had not shown up in the aerial photographs, they were withdrawn, leaving the infantry in possession of the Station yard but with the Hummocks still occupied by the enemy. Ordered to hang on, and unable to be supported, the infantry was screened by smoke. The artillery stocks of this type of ammunition had to be supplemented by regular trips to dumps twenty-five miles and more to the rear; the gunners of one battery were expending a three-tonner load every eight minutes, a rate which was exhausting to the crews and difficult to maintain.

Despite the best efforts of the artillery, the Germans were able to push the remaining Maoris out of the town. Using the smoke-screen to their own advantage, they infiltrated infantry and tanks, two of which overran Kiwi sections in the Station. Under fire from the tanks' 75mm

The Roundhouse and (right) the Hummocks, from the railway.
New Zealand Electronic Text Centre

guns and their machineguns, the seventy-odd New Zealand survivors, of the 200 who had attacked during the night, withdrew.

There was now a comparative lull in the fighting, with both sides consolidating their positions, and the Allies waiting for the weather to improve before launching their next attack, which was to be preceded by bombing Cassino town itself. Operation DICKINS was scheduled for 24 February 1944, but the winter weather, overcast and raining, delayed matters until 15 March. During this time the Germans replaced the troops from *15th Panzer Division* on the Cassino features with those from *1st Parachute Division*.

On the fringes of the town, New Zealand troops occupied isolated outposts in cellars and ruins of buildings, a disagreeable existence, one shared with the Americans whom they relieved:

> *As we trudged in through the mud-clogged fields on the dismal night of February 21st 1944, one of the boys asked the Yanks as they hurried past in the darkness "What's it like in there?" "Waal," replied one, who took time off to answer, "it's a hot old time in that old town", a reply regarded very shortly afterwards by A Company as "a gem of understatement"...*
>
> *The position held by the battalion was unusual and unpleasant. The forward defended localities of A and B Companies were within a few yards of the enemy, whose voices and movements could be distinctly heard. The enemy in positions on Castle Hill commanded all the forward positions held by both battalions and frequently swept them with machine-gun fire.* 25 NZ Battalion History

Many of the positions were under direct observation from the slopes

The Pasquale Road. The New Zealand infantry advanced down this road and Caruso Road, running along the foot of the mountains on the right, during the Third Battle of Cassino.
New Zealand Electronic Text Centre

The view from north of Cassino today, compare with the historical photograph below left. Author

above, and artillery and mortar fire was regularly brought down upon them. Aggressive patrolling, the use of rifle grenades and snipers exacerbated the risks. To add to the generally distasteful and unsanitary atmosphere, the smell of decomposing bodies, human and animal, which it was impossible to bury, pervaded the area. Despite the danger and appalling conditions, at least one group of Italians was discovered sheltering in a cellar, having endured the battles that raged above their heads for eighty days. They, and others, were evacuated by the Kiwis.

The Third Battle.

The focus of the fighting for Cassino town now turned to its northern edge. You will recall from the overview of the battles given earlier in this book that General Freyberg's intent was to capture the town from the north and then to secure river crossings into the Liri valley. Again, the northern edge of Cassino today bears little relation to its condition in early 1944, having had to be completely rebuilt after the war. The events of the Third Battle contributed in no small way to this state of affairs, for between 0830 and 1200 hours on 15 March 1944, 992 tons of bombs were dropped on the town, followed by an eight-hour artillery

New Zealand infantry in the town.
Associazone Battaglia di Cassino

barrage during which nearly 200,000 rounds added to the destruction.

In preparation for this, the Kiwis pulled their men back from their positions at the edge of town, except for a small covering force in the quarry, which remained in position until fifteen minutes before the aerial bombardment. As the artillery barrage started, 25 New Zealand Battalion advanced astride the Caruso Road, led by a squadron of Sherman tanks from 19 NZ Armoured Regiment. Indian troops on the slopes above the town to the west would give as much covering fire as possible. The New Zealand battalion objective was to capture that part of the town north of Route 6, with B Company to clear as far as the Continental Hotel, A Company to clear Route 6 eastwards to the Convent, with C Company mopping up. D Company was given the task of capturing Castle Hill (Point 193), which would then be handed over to a unit of 4th Indian Division.

As 25 NZ Battalion began its move into the town, there was practically no enemy fire, the defenders having suffered heavy casualties from the bombing and artillery bombardment that preceded the Kiwis' advance. B Company followed the Caruso Road, with A Company moving down the Rapido River beside it. Under cover of the barrage and a smoke screen they regained their old positions with little difficulty, but on advancing further into the town they soon came under machinegun and sniper fire from the ruins of buildings and from the slopes of Castle Hill. It became apparent that not only had the Germans not been destroyed, they were far from being demoralised and were still full of fight. Just over an hour after the advance commenced, the New Zealand companies lost contact with each other and with battalion headquarters. The tanks were delayed by bomb craters and had to struggle through debris to move forward, an eventuality which should have been expected, given the weight of bombs and shells which had been dropped onto the town. B Company, which should have cleared the town below the mountain slopes as far as the Hotel Continental, was forced away from the base of the hillside, into the town. It got as far as the ruins of a school, about 350 yards short of the objective, a delay which held up the advance of D Company on its way to attack the Castle.

It was intended that D Company would take Castle Hill from the south east after the town buildings at its base had been cleared by B Company. As this had not been achieved Major Hewitt, OC 'D', moved his company up the slopes towards Point 175 north of the Castle, and then down into the ravine between the two heights. 16 Platoon was tasked with taking Point 165, near the hairpin bend southwest of the Castle, while the 17 and 18 Platoons attacked up the ridge which leads

German mortars. Associazone Battaglia di Cassino

Castle Hill - Rocca Janula – from the town streets in 1944. Polish Institute

A New Zealand tank in the ruins of Cassino. Associazone Battaglia di Cassino

to the Castle from the east. We shall look at the events which followed there when we come to overlook the Castle from above, but it is worth looking up from the streets below now at the climb the Kiwis had to make to get to the top of Castle Hill, and to remember that their advance was made under machinegun and sniper fire from houses in the town.

Meanwhile, in the streets – or remnants of them – below, B Company was stalled. When his platoon commander was wounded, Sergeant Tulloch took command, despite being wounded himself by grenade splinters. By this stage in the fighting the platoon had been reduced to twelve men, but he arranged for tank support to shoot his small group forward as they attacked a strongpoint in some houses at the base of Castle Hill, about seventy-five yards away. Driven back by the enemy, he then established a position to one flank from where he was able to partly neutralise the strongpoint. Tulloch eventually had to be ordered to an aid point; for his aggressive tactics and personal example, he was later awarded the Distinguished Conduct Medal.

The bombing had so comprehensively destroyed the town buildings that the supporting tanks of 7 Troop, 19 NZ Armoured Regiment, already delayed by the cratered roads, could progress little further than the south end of the Caruso Road, some 600 yards from the Continental Hotel. 8 Troop penetrated into the town past the nunnery and the gaol, the crew members sometimes having to clear rubble from the route with shovels. Such was the confusion that they were unaware of the infantry positions and shelled houses that had been occupied by the Kiwis.

Just after nightfall, the rain began to fall heavily. It continued without respite throughout the hours of darkness, and with sodden clouds obscuring the moon visibility dropped to zero. Operations in these conditions, among the water-filled craters, could not be planned and executed. Without hot food and soaked to the skin, the men spent an uncomfortable night.

By the end of the following day most of the town was occupied, albeit with pockets of German resistance, but the south-west of Cassino, the vital area which had to be cleared to open the way to the Liri Valley, was still firmly held by the enemy. On 17 March 25 NZ Battalion, having cleared the Botanical Gardens in the centre of town, was halted by the paratroops in the Continental Hotel and the other strongpoints along the foot of the massif. 26 NZ Battalion should have, by now, occupied the Railway Station, but was unable to do so, and 28 (Maori) Battalion was ordered up to close the gap between 25 and 26 Battalions which had opened astride Route 6. The Maoris were then to clear the Hotel Continental and then the Hotel des Roses, with troops from 4th Indian Division working along the slopes above them to cover their western flank. This tactic, it was hoped, would permit the sappers to repair Route 6 so that tanks might push through towards Sant' Angelo.

As so often in the battles for Cassino, events took a turn for the worse, as the CO of 28 (Maori) Battalion commenced his planning using aerial photographs which were now rendered useless because of the heavy bombing. Landmarks had been obliterated and were unrecognisable, and in the cellars and ruins were parties of paratroopers. Two German tanks were concealed in houses close to the Maoris' start line on the edge of the Botanical Gardens. Others were spread throughout the area – one was in the row of buildings next to 21 NZ Battalion Headquarters.

As the attack moved off, the leading troops found themselves in a deadly game of hide-and-seek, where no sooner had one German machinegun nest been cleared than another opened up on them. In the face of this resistance and confused in the unrecognisable terrain the Kiwis ground to a halt. 'We had no idea whether we had reached our objective or how far we were from it as the area we were in was bomb holes and rubble and only parts of buildings standing.' (Second Lieutenant Waititi).

The net result of the operation was a partial clearance of the triangle between Route 6 and the base of the massif, but the Continental Hotel was still in German hands. New Zealand tanks were able to silence German tanks near the hotel, but could not advance further than the Botanical Gardens, and the battle became an exchange of artillery and mortar fire, with both sides laying down fire on their opponents. The infantry on both sides took to the cellars and concentrated on winkling out each other in close-quarter fighting.

21 NZ Battalion was the last to be thrown into the battle, moving into Cassino and attacking along Route 6 on the night of 20-21 March; but again it was halted by the defenders of the Hotel Continental and other strongpoints nearby. It was decided to hold the line from the Railway Station to Castle Hill for the time being, and no further attacks were attempted.

Attacks ceased – hostilities continued

Fighting in Cassino became a close-range slogging match amongst the ruins and shellholes, with only limited use of tanks being possible. Troops from both sides dug into the rubble and existed cheek-by-jowl with the enemy. The following excerpt from the history of 25 New Zealand Battalion illustrates the realities:

7 Platoon (Lt B. Simpson), 12 strong at this stage (and

Entrance to Maori Battalion RAP in crypt at Cassino. New Zealand Electronic Text Centre

A German tank below Castle Hill. The Monastery is in the background, and the steep slope up which the Kiwis climbed to capture the Castle is to its right. Gurkha Museum

German troops in the Continental Hotel. Associazone Battaglia di Cassino

mostly 3 Section under Corporal J. Wootton) shared a house with the enemy for three days, and for 36 hours lived on iron rations and cigarettes. On the second night a ration party got through with supplies of bread etc.... Unfortunately, early next morning as the platoon was preparing its first meal for two days, the enemy became extremely awkward.

Although the platoon had visibility from the front of the house, and some protection on the right side from 8 Platoon, the other two sides of the house were 18 inch solid stone walls with no holes or windows. While the Germans could be heard moving

British prisoners in the Continental Hotel.

about on the roof and next door, nothing could be done as all exits were covered by a German strongpoint across the street in front and grenade-dropping snipers on the roof. This meant that the only doorway – that into the water-covered alleyway between 7 and 8 Platoon houses – was effectively blocked.

With movement so restricted 7 Platoon were confined to a largely defensive role but even so accounted for a dozen or more of the enemy who were noisy or careless in their movements in front of the house at night. An attempt was made at one stage to pick a hole in one wall to provide communication with 8 Platoon but this proved impossible.

Back to the long awaited meal – about mid-morning as the food was being prepared, a quick aggressive Kiwi sentry lured three Germans into the house and so into the bag. These prisoners were not by any means arrogant or sullen. They were just plain scared – but not of us – and would not talk. After a while they were made to run the gauntlet across the alley and so handed over to 8 Platoon's care.

It was not long after that that the reason for a mysterious tapping in one wall, of the night before, was felt.

Before most of the platoon had time to eat anything, over half the ceiling and back wall were blown into the room with a noise in keeping with the damage. Yes, you're right, a demolition charge had been placed high up on the back wall. Fortunately, the platoon organized quickly, and the hole in the roof, the front of the house and the flooded alleyway were quickly covered. Attempts to rush the house were discouraged by lobbing grenades through the hole in the roof, and down into the alleyway. Meanwhile two inspired members of the platoon managed to pick a hole in the wall and provide an escape route into 8 Platoon's house. After sharing a nervy day with 8 Platoon, the two platoons were ordered to withdraw that night. This was done without incident and both platoons took part in a local attack carried out by A Company.

This episode was fairly typical of conditions in Cassino at the time. Platoons, often only a section strong, fighting well toward their objective only to be temporarily isolated. Their desired aggressive role was thus handicapped by shortage of manpower and so firepower and lack of communication to call for supporting fire.

25 NZ Battalion History

Paratrooper in the ruins.
Associazone Battaglia di Cassino

This state of affairs, of course, was equally applicable to the German troops holding onto the southern end of the town. The Kiwis learnt from prisoners that their enemy came from *3 Parachute Regiment*, having under command a battalion of *1 Parachute Regiment*, a *nebelwerfer* regiment, a machinegun battalion, and an anti-aircraft machinegun battalion. To augment this manpower were some seventeen to twenty *flammenwerfers* with ample fuel, seven or eight tanks, and the same number of self-propelled guns. The Germans preferred hand-held hollow-charged antitank weapons and grenades to antitank guns in the close-quarter fighting of the town.

The Kiwis also had tanks in the town. During the hours of daylight the crews had to remain silently inside the cramped confines of their vehicles, putting out the message that the Shermans which dotted the

An MG42 nest among the ruins of Cassino.

streets were abandoned hulks which had been destroyed in the fighting.

At night the tanks in Cassino acted as a sort of welfare centre for the infantry in the town: the crews would brew tea for them, hand out any food they had to spare, or help to bury their dead. All the time the tanks were on call should the enemy attack.

The troop commander's post was with the infantry headquarters in the crypt at the rear of the convent. A wireless operator with him was in contact with the tanks in the town and with RHQ, which was on continuous wireless watch ready to call up the squadron's reserve troop near the cemetery, just over a mile away.

20 NZ Battalion and Regiment History

On the night of 5-6 April, units from 1 Guards Infantry Brigade relieved the Kiwis in Cassino, and a period of sustained sniping, tunnelling, and general close-quarter action started. The Allies were waiting for the weather to turn dryer, and were amassing their forces for Operation DIADEM, and no major initiatives were planned before they were ready to launch the main assault. For the troops in Cassino, however, life continued to present a daily grind of continual danger and unpleasantness. Merely existing in the destroyed town, being unable to move during the hours of daylight, and surrounded by the decaying bodies of those who had died in the preceding weeks and months, called for a resolve which taxed the strongest character.

The following are excerpts from the handover notes given to Major Michael Gibson-Horrocks, 2 Royal Fusiliers, on taking over a sector in Cassino town from the Welsh Guards. They were written during the hours of daylight, when movement was impossible, and the author had time on his hands. They give a good picture of conditions in the town before the Fourth Battle:

Subject Rt Fwd Coy, Rt Sectn Area, Cassino.
To OC Incoming Coy
From OC 4 Coy, 3 Welsh Gds.

I hope these few notes will be of some help to you. I will try to make them as clear as possible. The Coy Area is held by Rt Fwd Pl (11 Pl 3 WG), Centre Fwd Pl, less 1 Sec (10 Pl 3 WG) and Left Fwd Pl (12 Pl 3 WG), with Coy HQ & 1 Sec (from centre Pl) back. So it's a three up position. The Pl areas are roughly 150x [yards] apart,

Page from handover notes, courtesy Michael Gibson-Horrocks.

and the Pls are about 200x or more from Coy HQ. The Pl areas are in either 1 house, or 2 adjacent ones. To cover the ground in between them, is impossible by fire, owing to the appalling state of the town (rubble, etc.) But they can be covered by sound, and anyone coming thro' the position should be heard, unless the stonk is heavy. The field of fire, in the Pl areas, varies from 2 yds to 30 yds. In view of this, the vital weapon, I think, is the TSMG [Thompson Sub Machinegun], tho' LMGs [Light Machineguns] should be brought up. The restricted view & continual darkness through day & night, in some of the areas, is a tremendous strain on the men. The Left Fwd Pl is especially bad in this way. With this Pl, the Kraut is very accurate with his Rifle Grenade, at times managing to put them thro' the loopholes. Owing to the nature of the ground, he is also apt to appear round a corner, about 5x away! Which causes intense excitement. As far as command goes, the Left Fwd Pl must, we think, have an officer. The Centre Pl is a simple task, and quiet. The

112

Rt Fwd Pl, although fairly peaceful, has rather a responsible job, in covering the L of C to Castle Hill. This Pl provides a standing patrol nightly, on the track to C.H. (about 100x from the Pl house). With Castle Hill so close, one can appreciate the difficulty at night. With porters and relief Pls going up nightly, there are a great number of people wandering about.

The Pls in their houses can hear all this, but can never be sure, whether the sounds are our people or Germans. In cases of doubt, we have sent out patrols from the Pl 'fortresses', to investigate these people. The stonk by day tends to be erratic, but rather sudden. At night, from 2100 hrs – 2300 hrs, it is heavy; and then lightens, until about 0400 hrs – daylight. Your Coy HQ is, I'm afraid, a German D.F. [Defensive Fire] task! It comes down at dusk, midnight & dawn. I think he knows the waterpoint is in the next door house. The mortars shake the place up, and bring down clouds of dust & muck; but do no other harm to people inside the house. An 88mm would, I think, go thro' the place.

Bn HQ is extremely close to Coy HQ, about 50 yds. Communications are doubled to all Pls, Line & W/T – with Line & W/T to Bn HQ. The Line gets cut regularly, & can only be repaired by night. If it goes, we immediately open on W/T. Or rather, that's the idea, but it doesn't always happen! There can be no movement whatsoever, by day. Here roughly is a plan of the position.

We have an internal Coy Net, each PL having a 38 set, netted to a Coy HQ, 48 set...

Adm All Pls are self supporting. They fetch their own water & rations, on Everest packs. An endless supply of candles, Hurricane lamps and Paraffin is needed. They go back to Jeep Head by Pl parties, staggered. And the same way, for fetching water. This is controlled from Coy HQ according to the degree of stonk. The journey to the Jeep Head is about 800x – to the waterpoint next door to Coy HQ, about 200x. There are plenty of tins for water in each area, which we will leave for you. Coy HQ, for instance, has 18 gallons/day. Cooking is on Tommy burners & petrol & wood...

S.B.s Stretcher Bearers are farmed out to Pls. They should have Morphia, as people cannot be evacuated until dark.

Obviously, the more TSMGs that can be stolen, or got from drivers etc., the better.

About visiting Pls. – however awful the crisis, I think there's little chance of getting to them by daylight – I go round them once during the night. A tiring business, as the going is appalling in the dark.

113

The extent of the devastation of the town of Cassino may be gathered from this picture of British troops passing through the streets.

Every man needs daps (gym shoes). Could this please be so for the takeover. It is all important, they should be worn for this. And for any movement out of the position for rations etc., when you're here...

Refuse We bury our tins etc. by night, near the Pl houses.

Latrines A quantity of lime is needed. I'll leave a latrine bucket

at Coy HQ for you. This is emptied at night & limed & dug. The Pls
improvise with amn. boxes etc.

Smell The smell in this town is revolting.

Tanks There are a number of dead Shermans scattered about.
We've had all the rations out of them! And the clocks. The Germans
are said to have booby trapped them – I don't think so.

Periscope Each Pl area & Coy HQ have these – we will leave them for you.

Sandbags Continual improvements can be made to the houses. They are always being knocked about & are inclined to fall down. A lot of Coy HQ came down today...

Arty Support This is done thro' Bn HQ by simply giving the number of the house to be stonked, from the aerial photograph – the same for mortar fire. Fwd Pls can always ask for it to Coy HQ: simply "Stonk 41B" or "Stonk 40". Fwd Pls should be warned when it's coming down, as it's extremely close to them.

Germans He seems to be good troops, rarely shows himself, and is good with the mortars. He had the incredible cheek, yesterday, on Hitler's birthday, to hang NAZI flags in the window of some houses. His Rifle Grenade is extremely accurate, the bastard.

I think that's about all – I apologise for this my screed!

Yours,

James Cull   21 Apr 44   4 Coy TAC

During the Fourth Battle, the troops in Cassino town tied down the German defenders. The main attacks of Operation DIADEM bypassed the area.

Cassino – the remains.
Associazone Battaglia di Cassino

Chapter Seven

HAIRPIN BEND Stand 7.

Drive up the road towards the Monastery, continuing **past the bend beside the Castle** and up past the next hairpin bend overlooking it, to **the right-hand bend where there is space to park a car.** Walk back down the road to the bend overlooking the Castle. The Castle is built on Rocca Janula, and features in some accounts of the battle under that name. You are now standing at Point 236. The bend beneath you, beside the Castle, is Point 165. All of these features were to play important parts in the battles.

The Castle was a New Zealand objective during the Third Battle. Possession of it gave a commanding position above the town, provided a foothold some way up the slopes which led to the Monastery, and it could be used as a launching point for attacks both upwards and onto the strongholds of the Hotels and Baron's Palace from above. From the hairpin bend the view across the town includes Route 6 (one of the 'Mad Miles'), Trocchio, and the line of the railway can be traced

The Castle from Point 236. The slope up which men of 16 Platoon, 25 NZ Battalion climbed to attack it is to the left of the lower hairpin bend, Point 165. See page 125 for a comparison. Author

Cassino town from Point 236 – the Hairpin bend. Route 6 runs from the centre bottom of the photograph before bending to the right and going behind Monte Trocchio. The Continental Hotel was in the dead ground beneath you, where Route 6 meets the foot of the slope. Author

running across the valley.

When the New Zealanders advanced into Cassino down the Caruso and Parallel Roads on 15 March, D Company of 25 NZ Battalion was detached to seize the Castle. As recounted in the narrative for Stand 6, the failure of the rest of the battalion to clear the Germans from the base of the slopes overlooking the town meant that D Company could not move to its intended position from whence to launch its attack. Major Hewitt, the OC, had to revise his plans and moved the company forward along the hillside from the direction of Point 175 and into the ravine to the north of Castle Hill. 16 Platoon was tasked with attacking up the sheer slope to capture Point 165, immediately above the hairpin bend next to the Castle, while 17 and 18 Platoons were to climb the hill from the east, 17 advancing on the right, up the ridgeline running from the town to the summit, 18 Platoon on the left and following a stone wall which ran to the Castle. With grenades and a Tommy-gun, a section from 18 Platoon fought its way upwards, dealing with German snipers and machinegunners in dugouts but losing all but three men in the process. Pinned down by a Spandau, the three had to wait an hour for the rest of the platoon before being able to move on to the Castle. 17 Platoon moved up its ridge to the Castle and the two platoons occupied the broken walls. After an exchange of fire and grenades being lobbed into a hole, the Germans defenders surrendered, the final

The Castle from Cassino town. 18 Platoon advanced on the left of the wall running to the top of the hill, under fire from Germans in the houses below.
Courtesy of the Polish Insitute

resistance ceasing by 1645 hours.

In its attack up the cliff-face to Point 165, 16 Platoon had set off at about 1300 hours. About 100 feet from the summit, Privates McNiece and Stockwell with a Bren gun were sent to the right to cover the advance. The German sentries, deep in their shelters because of the barrage, failed to notice the Kiwi attack and were taken by surprise, and those defending a pillbox on the crest were rushed by the two men. Stockwell subdued the pill box' Spandau with rifle fire and McNiece tossed grenades through the firing slit before opening up with his Bren through the aperture. Despite some resistance – the Germans threw their own grenades at the attackers, the explosion of one of which ruptured McNiece's eardrums – the twenty-five paratroops in the pillbox and a bunker beneath it surrendered, having lost two killed and five wounded. McNiece and Stockwell were both awarded the Military Medal.

Meanwhile the Germans on the hillside had come to life and brought rifle-grenades and mortar bombs down onto the platoon as it moved on to the Castle. For the cost of six killed and sixteen wounded, D Company had taken its objective; German losses were heavier, and included some forty-seven taken prisoner. The attack on Castle Hill had required Major Hewitt to devise and execute a completely new plan, once he had discovered that B Company's inability to clear his chosen line of approach had rendered the original one unworkable. He was awarded the Military Cross for this and later actions in Cassino.
The three platoons held the Castle until relieved at just after midnight by troops from 1/4 Essex Regiment. 5 Indian Infantry Brigade

German paratroopers armed with a MG 42 on the Cassino massif.

was to use the Castle as the start-point for their attack. They were to capture Point 236 (on which you stand) and then move along the slopes above the town to Hangman's Hill, from whence an assault would be launched onto the Monastery itself. One Essex company secured Point 165, the hairpin bend immediately adjacent to the Castle, and a sapper officer and his sergeant penetrated down the slopes to the rear of the Continental Hotel, reporting back that the German defences seemed poorly organised. For a while, things looked promising, but then defensive fire was brought down onto 1/6 Rajputana Rifles as they were moving up in support of the Essex, causing casualties. In the darkness and rain, two Rajput companies became dispersed and were pulled back; the other two joined the Essex company on Point 165. A further blow struck the battalion when its headquarters was hit by a shell which made casualties of all its officers, including the CO, Lieutenant Colonel West, and the adjutant.

Captain Drinkall (a later photograph).
Photograph courtesy the Gurkha Museum

The CO of 1/9 Gurkha Rifles then moved forward to assess the situation. Finding that only two of the Rajput companies were in position, he ordered up C and D Companies from his own battalion. Again luck was against them, for D Company ran into a group of the enemy armed with automatic weapons, and took fifteen casualties within a minute. The other company, under Captain Drinkall, was more fortunate. It reached the Castle without loss, and passed through towards Hangman's Hill.

The brigade now had only five of its companies on the battlefield – two from the Essex (the other two companies were garrisoning the Castle), two from the Rajputanis, and one Gurkha. Having helped the Essex to consolidate on Point 165, the Rajputanis moved against Point 236 at 0245 hours. The importance of the position should be apparent to anyone standing on it – from here the roads which must be used by attackers are under observation and the slopes of Monastery Hill are

Parachute Engineers. Associazone Battaglia di Cassino

dominated in both directions. Fire could be brought to bear on anyone attempting to bypass it either below or above.

The Germans had Point 236 well defended. When the Rajputanis advanced to within 150 yards of it, they came under withering fire and were forced back to the Castle to regroup. When dawn broke, the Essex and the Rajputanis were struggling to establish a perimeter around the Castle, and C Company of 1/9 Gurkhas had apparently disappeared – there whereabouts were unknown. At 0830 hours the Rajputanis again attempted – and again failed – to take Point 236. Once again the picture was looking gloomy.

From this position Hangman's Hill is out of sight, around the slopes to the south. There is not a convenient or safe spot on the winding road at which to stop to look at Hangman's Hill, although vehicle passengers will get glimpses of it as they drive towards the Monastery, so its story will be told here. Shortly after noon, reports were fed back to the brigade that figures had been seen on Hangman's, followed by a weak radio message. Captain Drinkall's C Company – the missing Gurkhas – was on its objective, having passed between the fighting for the hairpin bends above the Castle, and the Continental Hotel strongpoint below, en route to the rocky outcrop that would be the launching point for the Monastery assault.

It now became essential to support and reinforce the troops in this vital position. There were, however, three obstacles to consider before this could be achieved: Point 236 had still to be captured; the Hotel Continental defences posed a threat to anyone moving above them; and Point 202, an outcrop of rock lying close to the southernmost and lowest hairpin bend, had to be secured to stop the enemy interfering with movement to Hangman's Hill.

The New Zealanders took on the task of occupying the defenders of the Hotel Continental by putting in an attack, while the remaining two obstacles were to be an Indian responsibility. Two companies of Rajputana Rifles would again attack the hairpin bends from the Castle, while the remaining three companies of 1/9 Gurkha Rifles plus another two of Rajputanis would push across to Hangman's Hill. At Point 202, the Rajputs would storm or mask the feature to allow the Gurkhas to continue to their objective.

At 1900 hours the attacks on the hairpin and the Hotel went in. The Rajputanis succeeded in capturing the bend after three hours of fighting, although a strongpoint above it still held out. At the Continental, the New Zealand attack, although not taking the position, fully occupied the defenders and prevented them from interfering with the movements of the troops on the slopes above. The Gurkhas and Rajputanis slipped between the two fights, three hundred yards to either side of them, but encountered brief resistance from a party of Germans who were probably attempting to outflank the attack on the hairpin bend. As they moved onwards, they lost contact with the Rajputanis, but succeeded in establishing themselves on Hangman's Hill just in time to see off a counter-attack made on the position by German paratroops who rushed down on them from the Monastery. In dead ground below the summit, the Gurkhas were comparatively secure, but they could not remain there indefinitely.

In a similar fashion to their attack on Hangman's, at first light the Germans made a strong counterattack on the Rajputanis on Point 236, again driving them back to the lower hairpin beside the Castle.

The Gurkhas on Hangman's Hill were in dire need of resupply. C Company had been there for forty-eight hours, with only the food, water and ammunition that they had brought with them, and the other companies were only slightly better off. The task of helping them was becoming more difficult, however. Below them in the town, the German resistance continued unabated and it was becoming apparent that they had recognised that Castle Hill was critical to the outcome of the battle. Accordingly, they started infiltrating the area and attempted to establish a cordon around the Castle which would prevent it being used as a base from which to support the troops further up the slopes. From houses in the town, small-arms fire was brought to bear on anyone moving in the vicinity of the Castle, and a state of siege began.

In an attempt to get supplies to Hangman's Hill a field company of Sappers and Miners, with an Indian Pioneer company as porters, assembled behind Castle Hill. They had an escort from 4/6 Rajputana Rifles, and reached the Castle, heavily laden, at midnight. With

Air drop on Hangman's Hill. Associazone Battaglia di Cassino

German activity increasing, the decision was taken to leave the porters rather than expose them to further risk, and the Rajputanis shouldered the stores and moved off over the hillside, which by now was swept by fire. Aware of what was happening, the Germans launched a raid on Point 165, just 200 yards above the route of the supply party. Two Rajputani companies broke up this attack, but the rear of the supply column was hit by mortar fire, which inflicted casualties and caused some of the stores to be lost. The remainder pushed on to Hangman's Hill, where they were forced to remain, it being impossible to return in daylight. The situation on the rocky outcrop was becoming increasingly crowded and the problem of the shortage of supplies had been exacerbated by the presence of the extra men.

With the problem of resupply becoming critical, arrangements were made to attempt air drops. During the afternoon of 19 March, forty-eight aircraft dropped containers of water, food and ammunition; but with the dropping zone being so small, and on such a steep slope, many of the containers merely bounced down the hill and out of reach.

That night the contest for the Castle area resumed. The Essex made ready to expand the perimeter, but New Zealand tank fire which was intended to support them hit the Castle walls and the falling rubble buried several of the infantrymen. To add to their problems, German weapons firing on fixed lines sprayed the Castle entrance, making it impossible for more than one man at a time to sprint through. In spite of these hazards, a company of the Machine Gun Battalion of Rajputana Rifles got through to Hangman's Hill, and a company of 1/6 Rajputanas which had been there for the previous day returned with the wounded. Towards midnight 4/6 Rajputanas relieved the Essex in

124

the Castle, and two companies from the latter battalion moved up to reinforce the Gurkhas on Hangman's Hill while the other two were handing over the location to the Indians.

It was as dawn was beginning to break that the German paratroops launched an attack, charging down onto the Castle and the adjacent hairpin bend from the Monastery. Able to observe all moves below them, they were able to choose their time and objective perfectly, although the execution of their plan fell short in that the intention had been for another group to attack the Castle from the town, simultaneously. This second group was delayed in reaching the start line and its attack did not develop until later.

The Essex and Rajputana companies which were engaged in the hand-over process at the hairpin were over-run and destroyed by the paratroopers from the slopes above. The attack, like a medieval assault of old, swept up to the Castle walls, which the defenders manned with the aid of grenades and Tommy-gun fire at close range. Major Beckett of the Essex Regiment, and Major Oswald of 1 Field Regiment fought off the attackers with their men. After his comrades had been seen off, a German sergeant-major, a prisoner in the Castle who had watched the conflict with a professional eye was so impressed with the performance of the defenders that he presented Beckett with his fur-lined paratroop gloves as a token of his estimation. Throughout the battle, the behaviour of the German prisoners in the Castle had been noteworthy; all (bar the sergeant-major, who had elected to act as

The Castle in 1944   Polish Insitute

Fallschirmjäger **sniper.**

observer) had volunteered to become stretcher-bearers for the British wounded. One of them had even pushed Major Beckett out of the line of fire of a German sniper.

By 0800 hours the attack from above had been repelled, but an hour later the assault from the town commenced. With the Germans having fire control over the gateway, confused fighting followed. Another section of the wall collapsed, burying two officers and twenty men, before supporting mortar and machinegun fire from Indians and New Zealanders outside the Castle helped drive the attackers away.

For the two Essex companies en route to Hangman's Hill things went badly. Taking serious casualties, they arrived at their destination severely mauled and in no condition to assist in the final attack on the Monastery. Having arrived, the decision was taken to withdraw them, and the luckless group was forced to run the gauntlet of German fire again as it fell back down the hillside. A few managed to regain the comparative safety of the Castle, while the remaining survivors returned to Hangman's Hill. The battalion ceased to exist as a fighting force, and it was withdrawn from the fighting. 6 Royal West Kents was borrowed from 78th (British) Division to take its place.

Despite the inevitable delay while the West Kents were being brought into play, the Cavendish Road operation which was intended to draw off the Monastery defenders' attention went ahead, unsuccessfully (see Stand 10). At nightfall on 19 March 1944, the situation had deteriorated to a stalemate, with the initiative beginning to pass to the Germans. In Cassino itself, the New Zealand forces had yet to clear the town, and were engaged in close-quarter fighting in the house ruins. As an illustration of this, an Indian Advanced Dressing Station had to withdraw from the cellars of a building while New Zealand tanks dealt with German machine-gunners on the upper floors.

On Hangman's Hill itself, 1/9 Gurkhas had insufficient strength to drive home the planned attack on the Monastery, and an isolated New Zealand group was stuck on Point 202. The Hotel Continental was still a German stronghold, and the enemy controlled the approaches to the Castle. Nor was assistance from artillery or the Allied air forces of much use; the combatants were so closely intermingled that their power could not be brought to bear. On Hangman's Hill the smoke screen which was laid down to protect the Gurkha contingent proved less of a benefit than anticipated – the sangar in which the CO had established his command post received three direct hits by smoke shells, a factor which led to strained relations between the CO and the Forward Observation Officer, not least because the smoke proved worthless as it failed to hide one side from the other.

9th Gurkha Rifles. The regiment erected a memorial in the shape of this badge on Hangman's Hill. It no longer exists, but a replica is displayed in the CWG Cemetery.

It was becoming apparent that, until the bottleneck at the Castle was freed from German interference, the battle could progress no further. To facilitate this, Point 165 – the lower hairpin bend – had to be recaptured. The Royal West Kents were nominated for this task. 2/7 Gurkhas, from 11 Indian Brigade, would seize Point 445 after moving along the reverse, or northern, slopes of the ridge above the Castle.

As darkness fell on the evening of 20 March, two companies from the West Kents set out from the Castle. An enormous explosion occurred, the cause of which was never determined, causing many casualties in the leading company. The survivors were withdrawn to the Castle, where they reorganised before setting out again at 0330 hours. Meanwhile, however, the Germans had infiltrated machinegun teams to cover the Castle gate and to seal it so that the West Kent's attack had to be abandoned.

The Gurkha attempt on Point 445 was equally unsuccessful. The company which attempted it proved too weak for the task, and was withdrawn to allow the artillery to bring heavy fire onto the objective for the remainder of the night.

While these actions were taking place, German paratroops were making their own attacks on the supply route from the north, which had to be beaten back by companies from 2/7 Gurkhas and 4/6

Rajputana Rifles. Other paratroops infiltrated the gap between the hairpin bends and the Castle in an attempt to link up with the machine-gunners covering the Castle gate from the town ruins. As far as the Indians were concerned, the emphasis was now firmly on the defence, and it was determined to protect the route between the Castle and the supply dumps in the valley below with wire and mines. From the observation posts in the mountains above, this activity, like so many others, did not pass undetected, and an improvised force of German engineers launched an attack onto the Castle at dawn on 22 March.

The German side of this action, and those that preceeded it in the area above and around the Castle, is remembered by one of the paratroopers that took part in it, Lance Corporal Rudolf Valentin:

OPERATION OF 1ST PLATOON, 3RD COMPANY, 1ST BATTALION PARACHUTE ENGINEERS IN THE SECOND BATTLE AT MONTE CASSINO. [NB – German numbering of the Battle. To the Allies, this was the Third Battle. Kalvar Mountain is Point 593].

Gefreiter (Lance Corporal) Rudolf Valentin. Courtesy of Rudolf Valentin

At the beginning of the Second Cassino Battle 3 Company, under the command of Captain Jacobeit, was assault reserve and situated on the reverse slope of Colle San Angelo. We took up positions in crevasses and under overhanging rocks – not a comfortable position but safe from artillery and mortar fire. What, however, was not so good was having to fetch our rations and every drop of water from our supply point some 3 kms away on the Casilina Road, and then carry it up the mountain. On the way to and from the supply point we had to constantly reckon with artillery bombardment, as the enemy naturally knew that all supplies for the Cassino front had to come along this single route. When not assigned to this supply duty it was possible to enjoy the March sunshine.

With the air attack on 15 March this idyllic existence ended, however. 1 and

128

2 Platoons of our company were placed under command of the 1st Battalion of the 3rd Parachute Regiment commanded by Major Rudolf Boehmler and on the late afternoon of the 16th we were on our way, led by Captain Jacobeit. We passed the Massa Albaneta, progressed along the reverse slope of the Kalvar Mountain and then onto the monastery. On the way we were mortared twice but luckily suffered only two light casualties. On arrival at the monastery we reported to Major Boehmler and received our orders.

2 Platoon was ordered to attack the Indians, who had broken through and occupied the high Point 435 on Hangman's Hill from where they would be able to storm the monastery. 2 Platoon's objective was to recapture this point but due to the Gurkhas' superior numbers this was unsuccessful.

We of the 1st Platoon, 26 men under Corporal Saam, were ordered to clear both hairpin-bends, which were being defended by the Rajputanis and, if possible, to re-occupy Rocca Janula. At 0100hrs we left the monastery loaded down with ammunition and hand grenades, in order to carry out an attack in the early hours. Almost silently we edged our way downwards in the darkness and at about 0400hrs we reached the high Point 236 slightly above the upper bend and where the last 6 men of 3 Company 3rd Regiment were doggedly defending against the Rajputanis, who had worked their way to within 20 metres of this point. After a short briefing from Lieutenant Haering, officer commanding 3 Company, we attacked immediately but were met with heavy machinegun fire. Many of our grenades also hit tree stumps and came back at us. The second attack was however more successful. Two three-kilo charges thrown by Franz Draeger tore apart a machinegun position manned by the Indians and we immediately stormed into this gap firing our machineguns from the hip. The use of further high explosives enabled us to drive the Rajputanis from the lower hairpin bend. We then had to clear Point 192 to the left of us, which we managed, and pushed on to the saddle connecting Rocca Janula with the slope of Monte Cassino. Here we came to a halt. We remained under heavy defensive fire and as it was now becoming light we pulled back to Point 196 and the upper hairpin bend. We dug in here and covered the only connecting route leading to the Gurkhas on Point 435 with our machineguns. The heavy resistance that we had to overcome led to the conclusion that the

Indians were prepared to fight to the last man on Point 236 in order to keep the route free to Hangman's Hill and the monastery. With our assault group we helped speed up this plan. We did however pay the price for this action with two killed and two seriously injured. Our medical orderly, who was only about 20 metres from us, was captured by the Indians without us being able to intervene.

The position in which we found ourselves was not an enviable one. Seen from the monastery we were at the point of a very small wedge. To the left there was a very steep gorge, which ran from the monastery hill passing behind Rocca Janula to the town. This separated us from an Indian Brigade. In front of us was the castle and to the right and above us were the Gurkhas on Hangman's Hill. For this reason our movement during the day was very restricted. Whoever broke cover during the day was a victim of the Indian snipers or the English on Rocca Janula, not to mention the artillery as well as tank fire from the town, which would be directed against anything that moved on the hill. We were, however, given cover from the monastery, which lay high above us. The Gurkhas on Hangman's Hill were in a similar situation. During the day they too had to make themselves scarce otherwise they brought down well-directed German artillery and mortar fire from the monastery.

The whole situation meant that all attacks and counter attacks took place at night, which for our small number was an advantage. Immediately darkness fell we had to defend against the first attack, which on this particular night was followed by a further one. The enemy certainly did not want the door to the monastery, which was already nearly open, closed by our small contingent. The successful defence against these attacks was only possible due to changing our fire positions often, and the use of engineer explosive charges. At the start of the new day we had to creep back into the holes that we enlarged with the tips of our bayonets whilst we endured artillery and mortar fire. Then as soon as darkness fell the murderous close-quarter battle began again. We had to let the enemy approach within three to four metres before we could recognise him from the shape of his helmet. Furthermore hunger and thirst became an issue because the little water we had was reserved for the wounded, and then only issued in a dire emergency. To collect water or rations from the monastery was out of the question; everyone was needed

A German *Fallschirmjäger* operates an MP40 commonly refered to by the Allies as the 'Schmeisser'.

during these nights to defend against the fierce attacks.

In the early morning of the 19th or 20th March the 1st Battalion of 4 Parachute Regiment with a strength of approximately 180 men came to us from the monastery with the objective of recapturing Rocca Janula under any circumstances. After about 10 minutes the men of 4 Regiment overran the Rajputanis on the lower hairpin bend and stormed the walls of the castle, where terrible hand to hand combat broke out just like in the middle ages. The men attempted to scale the walls and they succeeded in blowing a hole in it. However, their opponents from the Essex Regiment who were defending the castle fought with the same doggedness and succeeded in driving back the attack, but with heavy losses. The courage and the readiness to make sacrifices of the men of 4 Regiment was of no use, the castle was not to be taken. Half of the men paid with their lives and the others had to withdraw to our positions. The English and the Indians, however, had also suffered such heavy casualties in this battle that they had to give up their aim of capturing the monastery through this route. On this day a ceasefire lasting

Both sides honoured the Red Cross flag and assisted each other in caring for the wounded.

Rudolf Valentin acted as a stretcher-bearer during this episode.

several hours was agreed to enable the dead and wounded to be recovered. This had not been possible during the days before. During this lull in the fighting we exchanged cigarettes with our opponents and they helped us with bandages. The English even lent us stretchers to take our casualties back to the monastery. The Gurkhas on the other side brought their wounded through our positions in the Rocca Janula. A short time later these men who had helped each other as comrades were once again the bitterest of enemies. What an irony!

Since we were now supported by the 1/4 it was possible to return to the monastery during the night to collect food, water and ammunition. In the following days the English attempted to supply the Indians, who were surrounded at Point 435 from the air. This was, though, unsuccessful, because the aircraft had to

Stretchering away British wounded.

drop their loads from too great a height and their parachuted supplies were blown towards us. Added to the trials of the previous days came a further plague and that was the smoke screen delivered by the English and American artillery to hinder our observation from the monastery. The smoke burnt our eyes terribly and caused coughing and breathing difficulties.

On the evening of the 24th March we engineers suffered the worst blow of this operation. An enemy artillery and mortar bombardment saw a shell hit the entrance to a small cave in which were 9 to 10 men of our platoon – all that was left of the platoon except for three men. The shock wave caused 20 hand grenades and a shell cartridge to detonate. The result was catastrophic – three dead and the rest seriously injured. The last three of our platoon, of which I was one, thanked our luck since we had already left to collect supplies. The next day during a renewed ceasefire we removed our injured comrades back to the monastery. Amongst the casualties were our platoon commander Stamm, and Franz Traeger, who unfortunately died a day later. He was buried by his comrades of 2 Company in the monastery yard at the foot of a palm tree that had been felled by enemy fire.

From the next day the Indians were to bring their wounded to the monastery and we assumed that they would also manage to take active men from Point 435 to the castle at the same time. However, they made a second journey to the castle and we let them pass, turning a blind eye – the same blind eye that came from having suffered the same experiences and grief as they had.

During the following night the few Gurkhas who were still on Hangman's Hill slipped past us on the Rocca Janula and we allowed this to happen. The next few days saw a further lull in the fighting and in the early half of April we three engineers left the mountain which had cost so much life, blood and sacrifice together with the men of Boehmler's battalion. Sappers Lang and Richter went for a few days rest and I, Lance Corporal Valentin, went to the field hospital in Fiuggi with malaria.

Both the Allies and the Germans were by now fought out. The Indian Division had lost some 4,000 men, and in the town below the last strongholds of German resistance proved impregnable. Despite Castle Hill being in Indian hands, the Monastery still remained inviolate. The offensive was abandoned on 23 March.

The problem of the Gurkhas on Hangman's Hill remained: it was imperative to pull them off the hillside as soon as possible. After the initial attempt to dislodge them, the Germans had tended to ignore the force, which became steadily weaker in the winter weather and with inadequate supplies.

Conditions grew steadily grimmer. Water had to be obtained from a puddle which was later found to contain the body of a mule, and food was strictly rationed. Casualties received only the most basic care under the prevailing conditions. Two medical orderlies from the Essex Regiment, Lance Corporal Hazle, DCM, and Lance Corporal Piper,

Castle Hill after the desperate fighting which took place over the slopes and summit.

treated all casualties from the resources of a first-aid haversack. Lance Corporal Hazel performed major operations, including amputations, with nothing more than a pocket-knife and a pair of scissors. His actions won him the much-deserved award of an immediate bar to his DCM.

Nor was Hazel alone in his heroism. It is almost invidious to select some instances above others, but one attracts the attention immediately: Baz Mir, a dhobi-whalla who – as a washer-man and camp-follower – had no combatant status, volunteered to act as a stretcher bearer when the field ambulance resources had been depleted by casualties. Having crossed a minefield under heavy fire, he made it to Hangman's Hill. The following day he repeated the journey, but on this occasion was intercepted by the enemy, who allowed him to proceed on his mission of mercy. He was awarded the Indian Distinguished Service Medal for his actions.

Communications were a major problem for the Gurkhas. Radio batteries had run down, and attempts to airdrop new ones had met with the same limited success as dropping other supplies – only four out of fifty replacements landed within the perimeter. To inform the Gurkhas of the decision to withdraw them, volunteers were called for from the officers of 5 Indian Brigade, who would commit the orders to memory lest they fell into German hands. During the night of 23/24 March, each equipped with a carrier pigeon, Captain Mallinson of the 1/4 Essex, Captain Normand of the 1/9 Gurkhas, and Lieutenant Jennings of the 4/6 Rajputana Rifles left the Castle at half-hourly intervals. (The three officers were, respectively, an Englishman, a Scot and a Welshman. Their pigeons were named St. George, St. Andrew and St. David). The first two of these officers reached the Gurkhas before dawn, giving the orders to withdraw upon receipt of the code word 'Roche'. At 1220 hours on 24 March the signal was radioed through, and the evacuation was made that night, with the distractions of a Royal West Kent raid from the Castle, feints by the New Zealand troops in the town, and artillery concentrations on the Monastery. Ten officers and 251 other ranks made it back safely after eight days on the hill, leaving some wounded to be evacuated the following day; the same night, the New Zealand company on Point 202 was withdrawn. The stretcher party bringing the last of the wounded down the hillside was given a message by a German patrol stating that no further facilities for evacuation of casualties under the terms of the Red Cross would be permitted.

Chapter Eight

THE MONASTERY Stand 8.

Drive up the road towards the Monastery. As you approach it, it is possible to see excavations on the slopes to the side of the road just before the top, which were dug by the Germans as shelters and supply points. To the right, down the hillside, is a road leading to the Polish Cemetery, which we will return to later. **Leave your vehicle in the car park** immediately in front of the Monastery entrance.

The Monastery itself has a long and distinguished history. Founded around 529 AD, it had a troubled past, being first destroyed by the Lombards in 577 AD, and again by the Saracens in 883 AD. Its bombing in 1944 became the subject of intense debate, which still continues. Looking at the building from the earlier stands it is apparent that it dominates the approaches to the Liri valley, and the Allied soldiers' belief that their every move was closely observed from its walls is readily understandable. As a defensive position, the whole of the Monte Cassino feature is extremely strong, even when faced with twentieth-century weapons. When it was originally constructed, it was virtually impregnable, and the site was used by the Italian Army between the World Wars as an exemplar of good defensive planning.

The importance of the Monastery was recognised internationally. The Italians had highlighted its value to the Allies well before the war had drawn close to it, along with other locations of great cultural and historical value, with the earnest plea that such places should be spared the ravages of war. Before departing to England to prepare for OVERLORD, Eisenhower had issued an order reminding his troops of Italy's contribution to civilization, and making the same point about avoiding destroying monuments of such irreplaceable worth. Nor did the recommendations to that effect stop there. In England, the Archbishop of Canterbury had made strenuous representations in the House of Lords to the same effect. Accordingly, Fifth Army had decreed that, if at all possible, the Monastery should be preserved.

Nonetheless, to the men on the ground, the Monastery presented an all-seeing, all-dominating feature which was an integral part of the defensive system of the Gustav Line. For many of them, it was impossible to separate the building from the mountain on which it stood, and although it was evident that the Germans would have observation posts all over the slopes overlooking the Rapido and Liri valleys, not merely on the most obvious place, it stood on the most important part of the ground. As much as anything, its menace was psychological, but it had to be removed as a military threat.

Major General Francis Tuker, GOC 4th Indian Division, was one of those who regarded the Monastery as an obstacle which had to be dealt with in order to open the road to Rome. Suffering from an illness which would shortly lead to his having to hand over command to Brigadier Dimoline, Tuker dwelt upon the problem and sought to research as much as possible about the building. The Allied intelligence branches had nothing, so he was forced to look elsewhere. The unlikely source of information on the Monastery's construction proved to be the book shops of Naples, in which details of the massive structure were unearthed. It was apparent to Tuker that it was a formidable objective, which – if not already occupied by the Germans – soon would be if they were to hold the position successfully. He began to lobby for its destruction.

The debate about whether the Germans had troops in the Monastery before the bombing has been resolved to most people's satisfaction: the authorities now consider that they did not. What is now apparent in hindsight, after the passage of over sixty years, was less so in 1944. Reports from Allied soldiers on the ground, and from General Ira Eaker, the senior Allied air commander in the Mediterranean Theatre, who had flown over the Monastery at low level, indicated that German troops were occupying it. In any event, if they were not there at the time of the reports, it was considered that they soon would be. They had cleared fields of fire from the surrounding area and were positioned so close to the walls as to make the question of the actual occupation of the structure almost academic.

The Germans had announced that the building was free of their soldiers and that it was to remain so. To this effect they had established an exclusion zone around it and placed military police on guard to enforce this ruling. On the other hand, they had also removed items of historical and religious value from the Monastery, an event which they used to the full for propaganda purposes, and advised the Abbot and his flock to leave. All but he and a handful of monks had done so, but the numbers in the Monastery had been swelled by over a hundred refugees who had been hiding in caves on the mountainside but who entered the building to shelter from the weather and the artillery fire which supported the 34th (US) Division as it attacked from the north, during the First Battle of Cassino.

The Germans were to reap another propaganda victory when the Monastery was bombed. As recounted earlier, on 15 February 1944 the building was subjected to a heavy bombardment which reduced it to debris. Although the intention may have been to deny its use to the

Germans as a stronghold, this objective was not achieved. Bombing it had given them the excuse they needed to occupy the ruins, which were now in a Stalingrad-like condition, a jumble of broken stones and masonry which provided an ideal defensive site. The cellars of the ruined building were turned into machinegun nests and mortar pits, little trace of which can be seen today. And the affect of its destruction on the morale of the attackers was largely undiminished.

Its military importance remained, however, and it was the objective of attacks in all four of the Cassino battles. These will be described in other chapters, but it is worth entering the Monastery and looking at the surrounding area from the defenders' perspective. Particularly good views may be had of Point 593 and, immediately below it, the Polish Cemetery. Beyond 593 the Polish Monument in the shape of a crucifix on Point 575 may be seen, and to the right of 593 is Snakeshead Ridge. The vulnerability of the Monastery to an enemy occupying Point 593 is self-evident. It is also worth looking down across the

Italian friends,

BEWARE!

We have until now been especially careful to avoid shelling the Monte Cassino Monastery. The Germans have known how to benefit from this. But now the fighting has swept closer and closer to its sacred precincts. The time has come when we must train our guns on the Monastery itself.

We give you warning so that you may save yourselves. We warn you urgently: Leave the Monastery. Leave it at once. Respect this warning. It is for your benefit.

THE FIFTH ARMY.

Pamphlet warning the civilian population of the impending bombing of the Monastery. It was – obviously – also printed in Italian.
Associazone Battaglia di Cassino

During the bombing of the Monastery.

After the bombing.
Associazone Battaglia di Cassin

Germans in the Monastery ruins.
Associazone Battaglia di Cassin

Poles inside the Monastery, May 1944.
Polish Institute

Group of wounded Germans with their captors.

141

The Polish Cemetery seen from the Monastery. The Monument on Point 593 is on the crest behind it, and Monte Cairo is behind the tree. In 1944 the ground was bare of such vegetation. Author

valleys of the Rapido and Liri Rivers to appreciate the command that this site gave over the routes the Allies had to take.

Apart from the unauthenticated Gurkha entry into the building during the Second Battle (which was mentioned earlier in this book) the attacks on the Monastery got little further than Point 593 and Hangman's Hill until the final days of the Fourth Battle when the Poles took 593.

Recognising that the position was no longer tenable, the German defenders slipped away leaving a number of their wounded in the ruins to be tended by the Allies.

Return down the road and take the turning to the left to the Polish Cemetery car park. Over 1,000 soldiers, casualties of the Italian campaign, are buried here, including General Anders and Archbishop Chaplain Gawlina, both of whom were buried here in 1970 in accordance with their personal wishes.

At the far end of the car park is the gate to the road leading to Point 593 and Albaneta Farm. The gate is normally locked, and the key has to be obtained from the Monastery.

Chapter Nine

POINT 593 Stand 9.

Point 593 was the objective for a series of attacks during the battles for Cassino. Today it is surmounted by the Polish Memorial, which is visible from miles around, from both the valleys of the Liri and the Rapido. The dominating position of the ground makes it clear why its possession was considered to be so vital, and even the post-war growth of trees around it, which today blocks the outlook towards Snakeshead Ridge in particular, does not completely hide the magnificent views from its summit.

Having gained admittance **through the gate into the Monastery grounds from the car park above the Polish Cemetery,** drive towards the crest of the hill, shortly before which there is a **turning to the right**, which should be taken. While not well surfaced, it is passable by car and leads ultimately to the Polish Memorial on Point 593. Just before reaching that position, there is another road which again branches off to the right towards a solitary house. This is Snakeshead Ridge, now covered with trees and foliage, the scene of heavy and prolonged fighting from the First to the Fourth Battles of Cassino. We shall return there after visiting Point 593.

Continue to drive up the hill before you, following it around to the left

A British 25-pounder crew shelling Cassino.

The Polish Memorial on Point 593. Author

to the small clearing which serves as a car park.

The Polish Memorial, which is sadly in a state of some decay, is a most imposing edifice. As you approach it from the small clearing below, the steps lead upwards to a platform on the side of which is inscribed the names of Polish soldiers who died during the Fourth Battle. The obelisk which surmounts the platform bears the following words:

> *For our freedom and yours*
> *We soldiers of Poland*
> *Gave*
> *Our soul to God*
> *Our life to the soil of Italy*
> *Our hearts to Poland*

Which sums it up – most movingly.

To the west of the obelisk, and set slightly below it, is a map-table constructed in cement which illustrates the lines of attack taken by the Poles in May 1944. Like the monument itself, it has suffered the ravages of time, and some of the features are missing. Nevertheless, it is a good spot to orientate yourself and to get a feel for the overall progression of the four battles from a German perspective. From here

View from Point 593 to the west. Monte Cairo is to the top right, and below it is Phantom Ridge, with the Polish Memorial on the left-hand hill, Point 575. Post-war buildings are in the valley, and the ruins of Albaneta Farm are just out of sight to the left. Author

and the other observation platform on the far side of the obelisk, good views are to be had of the Monastery and the Liri Valley.

On the southern side of the Memorial – the Liri Valley side – is an almost vertical drop. Albaneta Farm and the southern end of Cavendish Road can be seen below you where the ground levels out, the Farm now a battered edifice in a small group of trees. The southern end of Cavendish Road winds its way from the saddle to the right of the post-war farm buildings before running past the ruins of the old Farm, a solid structure standing amongst trees. It then proceeds below your viewpoint and beneath a vertical crag before most of it disappears out of sight en route towards the Monastery, to your left. Beyond the Farm and to the west is a cross on the crest of a prominent hill. This is another Polish Memorial, on Point 575, erected to commemorate the soldiers of the 5th Kresowa (Wilno and Lwow) Division. Further along the ridge on which it stands, to the right, is Colle Sant' Angelo. In front of this and on the far side of Cavendish Road, lies a lower range of hills, Phantom Ridge. Towering above it all is Monte Cairo.

Beneath you, in the crags of Point 593, may still be found remnants of the defences which the Germans constructed to defend this key place. Natural fissures and gaps in the rocks were expanded and the entrances reinforced with the aid of concrete to provide shelter from the Allied artillery and small-arms fire, and to build machinegun nests from which to shoot down the attackers.

A Polish soldier emerging from a German shelter in the Cairo massif. Every possible natural feature was used for defensive purposes.
Polish Institute

General Anders on Snakeshead Ridge. The Monastery is in the background. Polish Institute

hours on 12 May 1944. They captured the objective in a storm of aggression and reckless heroism, and moved forward towards Point 569, the next promontory towards the Monastery. The Poles took severe casualties in the attack, and the German defenders immediately counterattacked – twice – to push the Poles back and to attempt to retake Point 593. In the darkness on such rugged ground and at close-quarters, the battle was hard-fought but the Germans were unsuccessful. A third attack was mounted by a scratch force of company-size strength later, again without taking the Point, but the Germans went to ground in the crevasses and craters of its slopes and proceeded to snipe at the Carpathians, who were also subjected to a heavy mortar bombardment. As daylight faded at the close of the day, and under cover of the mortaring, the paratroopers rushed the surviving Polish troops and retook Point 593.

To the west, the Poles succeeded in reaching the northern end of the Albaneta massif, but were then pinned down by German artillery and mortar fire. 5 Wilno Brigade had advanced to clear Phantom Ridge, supported by a troop of tanks. Two battalions of 6 Lwow Brigade reached the foot of Phantom Ridge, under heavy fire which inflicted twenty per cent casualties. The Polish communications system became disrupted, and reports on the actual situation came back to the brigade commanders only intermittently. The attack lost momentum, and the tanks which had advanced with the infantry were unable to get far enough forward to assist. To make the situation even worse, when one battalion fell back, other troops took the action to mean a general withdrawal and joined in the retreat. Isolated companies from two battalions were left on the hillsides, and had to fall back from the Ridge later.

The impasse lasted for four days, with the Poles hanging on to their positions on Snakeshead while the Germans, with equal determination, held the Point. It was decided that they should delay any further attempts until XIII Corps had made more progress in the valley below.

During this period of relative stagnation, the Poles organised an artillery barrage which would cover future advances both on Snakeshead and on Phantom Ridges. Fighter-bombers attacked artillery positions behind the German lines. The Poles also hauled an antitank gun into a position on Snakeshead, from where it could deal with the enemy machineguns in the ruins of the Monastery, which had been bringing fire down onto the Ridge. Sappers worked to clear lanes through the minefields under cover of tanks, and the groundwork was

Polish casualty receiving first-aid. Polish Institute

152

generally put into place for further operations. Softening-up action was taken against the enemy. Under the barrage, the German defenders of Points 593 and 569 suffered heavily, with no means of evacuating the wounded. Emergency medical attention, including amputations, had to be carried out in the cramped shelters under fire from high-explosive and smoke shells.

On 16 May, at 2230 hours, the Poles tried again. 5th Division attacked on Phantom Ridge and succeeded in capturing most of Colle Sant' Angelo; and 3rd Carpathian Division once more advanced on Point 593. By 1130 hours on the following day, it was firmly in Polish hands. In both positions, the German paratroops reacted in their customary fashion, launching a series of counterattacks. On Colle Sant' Angelo ground changed possession several times, and – again – the Poles came under heavy mortar and artillery fire. But they held on, some of them being reduced to throwing rocks at the enemy because of shortages in ammunition.

On Point 593, the situation was little better. The Poles found it impossible to move forward, either onto the Monastery or towards Massa Albaneta. Despite heroic efforts to take the massif, the enemy held on grimly until the advance of Eighth Army troops into the Liri Valley threatened to cut off their line of retreat and they were ordered to withdraw. Despite their reluctance to surrender the ground which they had held so tenaciously for so long, the German paratroopers began to slip back towards the next line of defence, the Hitler Line. Many of them ran into Allied patrols and failed to take up their new positions, but a considerable number did manage to escape and to resist the advance towards Rome.

To look now at events earlier in the year, it is recommended that you **move down to Snakeshead Ridge**.

Snakeshead Ridge

From the Polish Memorial retrace your steps down the hill to the side road which you passed on your way up. Snakeshead Ridge stretches away to the north, and its importance becomes apparent once one has walked down the road towards the house, for it has a commanding view back towards the Monastery, although the trees now hide the views to the west. The house is occupied, and is private property. On its wall is a plaque commemorating the aid post which the Poles established on this site during the Fourth Battle.

In 1944, the ground was bare of vegetation, providing clear fields of fire for the defenders and no cover for the attackers. The rocks beneath one's feet are impossible to dig into, and any form of protection had to

German paratroops using a radio set on Monte Cassino.
Associazone Battaglia di Cassino

be built atop them, scanty low walls of stone and rubble – the sangars familiar to the Indian Army of former years on the North-West Frontier. On this ridge soldiers from many nations – German, American, British, Indian and Polish - were to fight and die, over a period of five months.

At the end of January 1944, troops from 34th (US) Division, having fought their way across the Rapido Valley floor to the lower slopes of

Polish soldiers examining German grenades. Note the harshness of the terrain, in which it was impossible to dig trenches. Polish Institute

Polish troops onthe massif. Casualties were heavy. Polish Institute

the Monte Cassino massif, pushed their way into the heights above them. 168 RCT advanced westwards through Caira, 133 RCT through the Barracks area on the Caruso Road and up onto Point 324 before turning southwards to Point 175 and on to Point 165 – the hairpin bend immediately above the Castle – before being forced back. 135 RCT operated on the slopes to the west of them, advancing (again unsuccessfully) from Point 324 to Point 445 before also being pushed back by the German *44th Infantry Division*, which was deployed in the area at that time.

In the face of these attacks, and those by the French further north, the Germans moved *211 Regiment* from the *71st Infantry Division* into the area, and alerted two battalions (*1 and 2/361*) of the *90th Panzer Grenadier Division* to follow it. They were in position by 1 February. The following day, *3/3 Parachute Regiment* also arrived from the Adriatic.

With 34th (US) Division now exhausted, the New Zealand Corps took its place on Snakeshead. 7 Brigade of 4th Indian Division moved onto the mountain slopes and began to replace the Americans. The story of the attacks made by 1st Battalion, the Royal Sussex, 4/6 Rajputana Rifles, and 1/9 and 1/2 Gurkhas was related earlier in this book. Standing on the Ridge and facing Point 593, you are on the route followed in their assaults by 1 Sussex on 15 February and the following night, and the Rajputs on the night of 17/18 February. Down the slopes

155

to your left, towards the Rapido valley, is the line of attack of 1/9 Gurkhas, the same night. Both battalions were driven off by the defenders of Point 593. Further down the slope again, 1/2 Gurkhas had moved directly towards the Monastery from a start line to your rear, further back along Snakeshead. You will recall that B and C Companies of this battalion ran into tripwires and mines in what they had assumed to be no more than a belt of low scrub which lay across their path, and suffered heavy casualties. Amongst the wounded was the Commanding Officer, Lieutenant Colonel Showers. Stretcher-Bearer Sher Bahadur Thapa crossed the scrub area no fewer than sixteen times to retrieve the wounded; he was killed shortly afterwards.

A and D Companies worked their way around to the left of the scrub and pushed on towards the Monastery, and eventually B Company established a foothold on Point 445. Three companies from 1/2 Gurkhas were now 800 yards from the Monastery, under heavy fire from three sides. As recounted earlier in this book, some of them may even have entered the building before being cut down. As dawn drew nearer, fighting was still taking place around Point 593 and the Gurkhas on 445 were trying to find cover amongst the rocks. It was necessary to withdraw them from their perilous position before the sunrise, which would have left them naked to the view of the Germans.

The men of 7 Indian Brigade now had to hold onto what precarious gains they had made, erecting sangars – 'digging in' being impossible – behind which they crouched in the winter weather, with snow, sleet and rain. The conditions under which they operated can be imagined. Huddled behind low stone walls and unable to expose themselves without bringing down a storm of bullets, grenades and mortar bombs, their existence was precarious. The enemy was no further than forty yards away, and the brigade suffered sixty casualties daily.

Bodies of the dead, men and mules alike, could not be recovered or buried in the impenetrable ground. The best that could be done for those that could be reached was to throw a shovelful of lime onto the corpse to hasten its decay, and to cover it with a groundsheet weighted down with rocks. Natural bodily functions had to be performed, often while lying flat behind the low walls, into ration tins which were then lobbed in the general direction of the enemy. The smell of rotting flesh, ordure and of exploding munitions produced a noxious cocktail which could only be described as stomach-churning; and which got progressively worse as warmer weather arrived later in the year.

Another facet of life on the mountain slopes was the problem of bringing supplies forward. Everything – water, food and ammunition – had to be brought firstly by mule and then manhandled up to the front lines. Hot meals, which would have given both nourishment and

Indian troops on Snakeshead Ridge. The Gurkha Museum

comfort to the exposed soldiers, were impossible for those in the forward positions. And conditions were only marginally better for the Germans who, at least, had the opportunity to prepare their defences with the assistance of explosives and concrete before the Allies arrived. Some of these positions may still be found on the hillsides, together with items of the more resilient detritus of war such as shrapnel fragments and rusted ration tins. Time – fortunately – has erased the smell.

In April the Ridge was taken over by 11 Brigade, from 78th Division. The other two brigades, 36 and 38, took over the Castle and the Caira area respectively. For the men of the battalions involved, the introduction to the area was less than welcoming. The slopes were no more hospitable to them than their predecessors, and as the weather began to warm up, the atmosphere became even more foetid. An ongoing problem was the difficulty in bringing fresh water forward, and a stagnant pool proved too tempting for some thirsty soldiers who fell prey to snipers.

The difficultes of supplying the front lines were not only experienced by the Allies. A German paratrooper leads a mule up the slopes.
Associazone Battaglia di Cassino

Chapter Ten

ALBANETA Stand 10.

Return down the road from Snakeshead, taking the right turn at the T-junction. The road from the crestline wends its way under the crags of Point 593 past a cave on the right-hand side, in which – as with every nook and cranny – the German defenders sheltered. There are a number of Polish direction stones along the route, commemorating the various units of that nation which fought here in 1944 and showing the way to further memorials.

Albaneta Farm, or more correctly its remains, lies to the left of the

Albaneta Farm in 1944. Polish Institute

road. The Farm was the objective of the 34th (US) Division's 135 Regiment on 7 February, when it was intended that this unit would capture the position and thus deny its use to the Germans who could bring flanking fire to bear on 168 Regiment as it attacked along the ridge from the east of Point 593 and over Points 444 and 445. Standing beside the Farm ruins it is easy to see that the Americans had a hopeless task in holding the area when the Germans were still in

MG 42 on the slopes overlooking Albaneta. Associazone Battaglia di Cassi
Albaneta Farm as seen from the German positions on Hill 593.

possession of the hills above the modern farm buildings to the west. Badly damaged by artillery and air strikes, the building was later used by the Germans as a medical post during the fighting.

From the Farm, continue to drive down the road, **going to the right** of the modern buildings and up through the saddle between Snakeshead and Phantom Ridges. Just on its far side is the remains of a Sherman tank which the Poles turned into a monument by raising a crucifix made from tank tracks on its turretless hull. The turret lies alongside it. On the plates which support the crucifix are inscribed the words 'To the heroes of 4th Polish Arm Regt who gave their lives marching to Poland' in Polish and English, and the names of the fallen. Like most of the Polish memorials, this one is again in poor repair.

Looking down the valley the northern route of Cavendish Road can be seen. It is possible to go further down the track, to the wider valley floor known in 1944 as Madras Circus, before the surface deteriorates sufficiently to make driving impossible, but **you may have difficulty in turning your vehicle for the return trip.** For the energetic, it is possible to walk the entire length of the road, right down to Caira village.

Standing beside the Sherman memorial, the difficulties encountered by the armoured columns which pushed along this road on 18 March 1944 can be appreciated – and the question asked of why such a desperate venture was permitted to proceed, without infantry support and when it was already apparent that the attack on the Monastery from Hangman's Hill – which it was designed to support – was not going to happen.

Cavendish Road offered a route around the west of the German defences facing the Rapido valley. Worked on by the Royal Indian Engineers' Sappers and Miners, an existing track from Caira village was widened and strengthened so that it might carry tanks as far as Madras Circus, a distance of about a mile and a half and rising 800 feet. The Germans seemed unaware that all of this effort was taking place, under cover of camouflage netting. Under conditions of great difficulty, the road was completed in time to permit a diversionary attack to draw the German defenders' attention away from the assault on the Monastery planned to be launched from Hangman's Hill. While the road led into the hollow between Snakeshead and Phantom Ridges, which should have given a covered approach almost to the Monastery walls, it was extremely unlikely that the Germans would not have it commanded by guns. Due to start the demonstration at 1600 hours on 18 March 1944, after the Hangman's Hill attack had been launched at

German paratroop and *Gebirgsjager* officers on the mountains overlooking Cassino. Associazone Battaglia di Cassino

dawn on the same day, it was clear by this time that the Gurkhas were not going to be able to carry out their part of the operation.

It is fair to say that the New Zealanders were unimpressed with the operation. The ground was unsuitable for tanks, there was no infantry support, and the force's commander, Colonel Grey, was an artilleryman with no experience of tanks. Nevertheless, it was ordered to proceed.

The columns of tanks – totalling fifteen Shermans from C Squadron of 20 NZ Armoured Regiment, twelve Stuarts of 760 US Tank Battalion, another five Stuarts from 7 Indian Brigade's Reconnaissance Squadron, and three American 105mm self-propelled guns – met at Madras Circus and then pushed down the road. One look at the ground on either side of the road will indicate the problems they faced. A tank, fortunately the last in the column, slipped off the narrow track on the way up the hill and became stuck. Three other tanks threw their tracks, either on the rocks or from detonating anti-personnel mines, and snipers kept up a steady fire on the commanders, most of whom found it necessary to keep their hatches open because of the rough going and the fumes from their own guns. German mortars were then brought to bear on the

New Zealand Shermans.

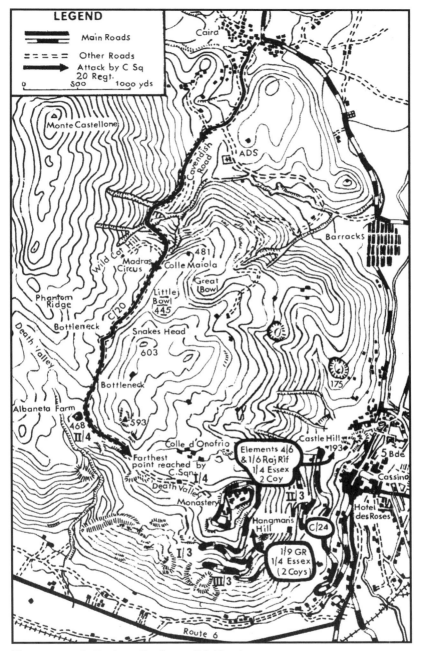

The armoured attack on the Cavendish Road.
New Zealand Electronic Text Centre

163

Polish tanks on the massif.
Polish Institute

column, setting equipment lashed onto the back of one tank afire. As they passed through the narrow gap between the hills on either side – near the Polish tank memorial – heavy artillery fire came down onto the leading tanks. As the Kiwis pushed through the bottleneck as fast as they could, some of the Americans and the Indian Reconnaissance Squadron attempted to clear the slopes of the Phantom Ridge and to move towards Point 575, to your west. The New Zealand official history states that 'they struck bad going' and a look at the ground they attempted to cross leaves one with a distinct feeling of understatement. All but one of the Indian tanks were put out of action, most losing tracks, and one American crew was taken prisoner. The attempt was abandoned, and the rest of the American tanks followed the New Zealanders towards Abaneta.

Breaking through the bottleneck, the leading Shermans opened fire on Albaneta Farm. It had already suffered considerable attention from artillery fire and bombing, and little resistance was experienced from that quarter. Turning their attention to the slopes of Point 593, the tank commanders began to search for German machinegun nests, but found that the Indian troops holding positions on Snakeshead were too close to their opponents for any useful assistance to be rendered by tank fire. Leaving two Shermans to maintain a watch on Albaneta, where some signs of life were still to be seen, Major Barton, commanding C

Stug III on the Italian Front.

Fallschirmjäger operating a PAK 38 anti-tank gun outside Cassino.

A Polish Sherman at the south end of Cavendish Road. This is now the Memorial.
Courtesy the Polish Institute

View from the other side of the same tank.
Courtesy the Polish Institute

Memorial to the Polish 4th Armoured Regiment. Author

Squadron, ordered a troop of tanks forward around the bend in the road to determine how close they could get to the Monastery. All this time, German artillery fire rained down upon them.

After an anxious wait, the troop commander's tank returned down the track, holed by German antitank weapons and with its commander dead. Lieutenant Renall had been shot through the head by a sniper. A second tank attempted to move up the track with equally futile success, most of the crew being killed or wounded, and a third got

American Stuart tank, of the type used in the rescue the Kiwi Sherman crew.

stuck on the flat ground past Albaneta, with casualties among its crewmembers. A motor had been disabled by enemy fire, and the tank had bellied on the edge of a bomb crater. Heavy fire smashed the tank periscopes and kept the crew battened down. Barton was reluctant to commit another tank – there were only three fully operational Shermans left to him – and was trying to put down smoke to allow the stricken tank's crew to make a dash for it, when two American Stuarts drove up and took the Kiwis aboard, the crewmen having had to bash their buckled hatches open with empty shell cases in order to effect their exit. For his part in this event, Lieutenant Chester M Wright, one of the American tank commanders, was awarded the MC.

A further attempt was made, this time by Second Lieutenant de Lautour, to get closer to the Monastery, but to no avail in the face of German resistance; and the American Stuarts lost seven of their number late in the afternoon when they tried to get around the southern shoulder of Point 593.

As the day drew to a close, the remaining five C Squadron Shermans were withdrawn to Madras Circus. Earlier in the day hope

German prisoners with their Polish guards. Polish Institute

had been raised in NZ Corps by an intercepted German radio message to the effect that eight tanks had broken through their defences and that an infantry attack was expected imminently from the rear. By 1020 hours, the Corps and Divisional Commanders agreed that should the tanks bring the Monastery under fire, then the Hangman's Hill attack would proceed – but they could not, and the attack did not go ahead. Now, faced with the unhappy prospect of holding ground at night without infantry support, and vulnerable to German tank-hunting parties, the decision was taken to pull back.

The tank advance along Cavendish Road had taken the Germans by surprise and had taken some of the pressure off the troops on Hangman's Hill. Whether it could have reached the Monastery is doubtful: the track may not have been wide enough for Shermans for its whole length, and several had already been disabled through throwing tracks on unsuitable ground. The furthest Kiwi tank penetrated as far as the cave at the side of the road beneath Point 593 which you passed on the way to Albaneta Farm. Any advance much further past this point would probably have required sapper assistance to render the road suitable.

The attack made little difference to the main battle for Cassino. It was essentially a raid which formed one arm of a pair of pincers; without the other arm it could achieve nothing. It was a courageous effort which, like so many others in the battles for Cassino, spoke highly for those who carried out – but to no avail. Among the decorations awarded for their part in the fight were five MCs (one to the commander of the Indian Reconnaissance Squadron, one to the Gunner OP officer, and three to Americans). Four MMs were also awarded, and Major Barton was recommended for the DSO, an award which was not made.

On the German side, initial nerves which were reflected in the intercepted radio message were replaced by the determination of the defenders to behave in their customary bravery. Paratroops engaged tanks with grenades and rifles, and one account credits them with destroying tanks by wrenching open the hatches and throwing mines inside. Most, however, were incapacitated by mechanical failure, thrown tracks, or becoming bogged down. The Germans were not slow to make capital of the mistakes made by their foes. A propaganda leaflet appeared which read, 'Many tanks of the 760th US Tank Battalion advanced without infantry support. Obviously, they thought that they could smash these Jerries single-handed. One out of ten has come back from the Monte Cassino, the others still lie up there knocked to pieces!'

Assembled at Madras Circus, the remnants of the force came under artillery fire but were otherwise not bothered by the enemy. The American and Indian tanks left on the night of 21/22 March, but the Kiwis stayed until the following day, when all but one troop was withdrawn. These remaining three tanks were left to support the Essex Regiment in the area. They stayed there until the beginning of April, with crew changes being effected every four days, but saw little action.

The Poles

As described on Point 593, the Poles took command of operations in the mountains in April 1944. Aiming to capture Point 593, Point 575 and Colle Sant' Angelo simultaneously, General Anders hoped to prevent the Germans from concentrating their forces to deal with a more limited threat, as they had done previously. In his favour, of course, was the fact that he, together with the other Allied troops brought together for Operation DICKENS, had sufficient troops at his disposal to mount all of these attacks at the same time.

The plan was, firstly, to isolate Monte Cassino and the Monastery from the north and then to push through to the Liri Valley to link up with XIII Corps, and then to capture the Monastery itself. By attacking Point 593 and Colle Sant' Angelo, the Germans would have to disperse their reserves; the Germans at the Monastery and on Monte Cairo would be kept under a heavy barrage and masked by smoke to prevent them from bringing observed artillery fire down on the Poles as they attacked.

Colle Sant'Angelo and Points 575 and 505 were to be captured by the 5th Kressowa Division; it would then bring fire to bear on the

Polish casualties being evacuated down the Cavendish Road by jeep.
Polish Institute

171

German forces in the Liri Valley and protect the rear of the 3rd Carpathian Division as it came into action against the Monastery. The Division would also hold Monte Castellone to cover the right flank of the Polish Corps. So as not to allow gaps to develop in the Polish line, it would not move beyond Phantom Ridge until the 3rd Carpathian Division had established itself on its first objective – Point 593.

The actions of the Poles were described earlier, and it would be repetitious to do so again here; nevertheless, it is worth looking at the terrain around you and reflecting upon the problems that they faced in fighting through this area during the days of May 1944.

The next Stand is in the village of Caira, which lies to the north of Cassino town. As the crow flies, the shortest way there is via Cavendish Road, but as this is impassable to vehicles, it is necessary to **retrace your steps back past the Polish Cemetery and the Monastery.**

Chapter Eleven

CAIRA Stand 11.

From the town of Cassino, **take the Caruso Road northwards** towards the village of Caira. The road runs past the quarry at the foot of the mountains which was used as a forward base by the American and New Zealand troops attacking the town during the First and Third Battles of Cassino. A little further north along the road is the site of the Italian Army Barracks, readily identifiable by the post-war military buildings which occupy a smaller site than their predecessors.

Between the quarry and the village of Caira is a shallow cutting in the steep slopes to the west, which was one of the routes into the mountains taken by the mule trains to deliver supplies to the troops on Snakeshead Ridge. The apparently simple process of getting to the forward positions was in itself often a major ordeal, particularly when the weather was inclement – and for at least half the nights in the months from December to March the temperatures dropped to below freezing. Even when it was less cold, the pouring rain not only made life miserable for the ill-equipped soldiers huddled in their scanty shelters, but it turned the ground into a quagmire, made worse by the

'Compo' rations arriving by truck. Sufficient food for fourteen men for one day.

To 'mule-head'. Supplies being moved forward.
Polish Institute

From 'mule-head' onwards – on the backs of soldiers.
Polish Institute

feet of men and the hooves of mules. On the valley floor, off-road movement by vehicles became virtually impossible. The conditions after a dry spell were particularly bad because the mud became more glutinous, requiring a physical effort to pull the foot free rather than merely lifting it from the sludge.

The logistic chain to the front-line troops consisted of, firstly, trucks to a point as far forward as was drivable and safe (which, given the position of German observation posts, was sometimes some considerable distance away); then by mule train, again to the last secure and practicable position; and finally by porters. Having received the supplies from the mule head, these men faced the ordeal of marching a considerable distance which almost invariably led to a climb of several hundred feet in the darkness. This they did while carrying heavy loads of munitions, equipment, food and water. Where possible, sleighs were employed to drag this weight forward, but mostly it was brought up on the backs of the porters, a task which was not only gruelling but endless.

At Cassino whole battalions were employed as porters, moving supplies forward and casualties back. Pioneers provided stretcher bearers well into the advanced locations, working for as many as seventy-two hours without sleep, and becoming like zombies. All of these men were aged over thirty, which was – compared with the youth of the infantrymen – regarded as being considerably ancient. With the harsh weather conditions and the extreme physical labour, many suffered badly.

The First Battle

To the east of the road, opposite the Barracks, is the ground that 34th (US) Division crossed in its advance into the massif. The plan had been to cross the Rapido and for 133 Regiment to capture the Barracks and Point 213, which is the high ground to the north, inside the bend of the road leading into Caira. The Rapido was more fordable here than further downstream, but it was still a major anti-tank obstacle, the more so because the river banks were sodden with water. The German defenders had planted a minefield some 300 yards deep on the western side of the river and removed all vestiges of cover from the flat valley floor. Along the base of the hills was a belt of machinegun nests and pillboxes, and self-propelled and anti-tank guns were concealed in fortified houses to cover likely routes forward. Protecting these was a fifteen-yard deep belt of barbed wire. And, of course, behind all of this were the hills with still more pillboxes, foxholes and machinegun nests, hidden in the broken and uninviting ground which aided the defender rather than the Americans.

A 75mm Pak 40 anti-tank self-propelled gun, known as the Marder III, hidden away in an Italian farm building.

The valley in winter. Tanks could only get through such country on roads.
Polish Institute

At 2200 hours on 24 January 1944, two battalions of 133 Regiment attacked across the Rapido, supported by tanks which attempted to blow a hole in the ridge of the far river bank with their main armament. By midnight on the following day, they had managed to secure a small bridgehead with one battalion, after suffering casualties from heavy German artillery and machinegun fire. On 26 January the Americans attempted to reinforce this group, but the tanks leading the advance became bogged down in the flooded ground and blocked the movement of those following. A single company from 1/135 Regiment got across the river that night, but it, too, was unable to move further forward.

Upstream 168 Regiment, with a platoon of tanks, forced a crossing on the morning of 27 January. Two tanks managed to make their way through the flooded banks to the far side by 0830 hours, followed by two more an hour later, but no more could cross because those that had done so had churned up the ground so badly as to make it impassable. The four tanks succeeded in pushing forward into the western bank, their tracks destroying anti-personnel mines as they did so, and providing cleared routes for the following infantry. They also broke passages through the barbed wire and laid down suppressing fire on the enemy machinegun posts – before they were all knocked out.

The infantry were able to get to the foot of Point 213 during the early hours of 28 January, but the company commander withdrew because he felt that the position would be untenable in daylight. The

The dreadful winter weather added to the benefit of the defenders. Movement of supplies was severely hampered.

withdrawal turned into a rout as troops nearby saw his men falling back, and they were only halted at the river. What few remained on the western bank had then to be pulled back because they had become too exposed.

To the north, General Clark had ordered General Juin's French Expeditionary Corps to change its line of advance through the mountains. The French had been moving on Atina, a direction which they believed would outflank the strong defences of the Gustav Line around Cassino. To protect the right flank of 34th (US) Division, however, Clark needed the Colle Belvedere range securely in Allied hands. To achieve this, the French had to cross both the Secco and Rapido Rivers before assaulting the 800 metre mountain, which was heavily defended and denuded of cover.

The attack was launched with the barest minimum of preparation because of Clark's urgent need for protection for 34th (US) Division. Juin's supply route, which was under constant German artillery fire, was a single mountain road. The men from 3rd Algerian Division who were to lead the assault, the third battalion of 4 Tunisian Tiralleur Regiment (3/4 RTT) had to carry everything forward, mostly in the hours of darkness to avoid being observed by the enemy. Fording the rivers, they began their attack on 25 January, on an objective which one of them described as being three times the height of the Eiffel Tower. Looking at the mountain, it is easy to see that they must have felt just as exposed as if they were doing precisely that. It took them eight hours to take the objective, but at great cost. To the battalion's south, 2/4 RTT had taken Point 700 only to be thrown back by a German counterattack. Falling back, they nevertheless hung on to the lower slopes, and the following day (26 January) the battalion again attacked, this time on a more north-westerly axis which took them to the right of Point 700 and up onto Colle Abate, which they reached at 0230 hours the next day, 27 January.

The fighting for the high ground continued until 31 January, with attack and counterattack progressing until the French succeeded in consolidating their gains, but at immense cost. Only thirty per cent of the strength of the assaulting companies returned.

On 29 January, their right flank covered following the advance onto the Colle Belvedere massif by the French Expeditionary Corps, 168 Regiment from 34th (US) Division launched its attack on Points 213 and 56 from across the Rapido. In preparing for this attack, the Division's engineers had laboured to strengthen the approaches by laying down logs to form a 'corduroy' road, and together with the better condition of the approaches, these enabled a dozen tanks to reach the infantry which had preceded them to the foot of the hills.

An American howitzer crew during a barrage.

American troops on the Cassino front, January 1944.
Associazone Battaglia di Cassino

With the tanks again pushing safe lanes through the mines and wire, all three battalions succeeded in seizing their objectives, which they found to be well-prepared for defence with elaborate bunkers and machinegun nests. The following day Caira fell to the Americans, despite German counterattacks.

The Barracks again came under American attack on 1 February, when 133 Regiment cleared them of enemy with the assistance of tanks. The regiment then moved down the road towards Cassino, with a company deployed on the ridge above it, until they encountered fierce resistance on the outskirts of the town. House-to-house fighting through buildings which had been fortified and turned into strongpoints ensued. With the Germans having good observation positions overlooking the area, heavy casualties were inflicted on the attacking GIs. In such circumstances tank support was limited, and the soldiers had to inch their way forward through the rubble using bazookas to blow holes in the walls. Grenades were an essential part of

Troops from 34th (US) Division with German prisoners.

Japanese Americans – the 'Nisei' bring in a wounded comrade.

the weaponry, and the battle was continued at very close range. The Japanese Americans – the 'Nisei' – of 100 Regiment, attempted to take the Castle from across the ravine to its north, but without success.

Caira Village
The road curves to the left and begins to rise as it enters the outskirts of the village of Caira. Signposted to the right is the **German Military Cemetery,** which is deserving of a visit. Containing over 20,000 graves,

the Germans suffered over 20,000 killed in the fighting around Cassino.

most under markers inscribed with two or more names, the cemetery has a different appearance and character than the Commonwealth Cemetery. Whereas the latter has the familiarity of an English churchyard, with flowers planted along the rows of headstones, the German cemetery is situated on a hillock with the graves rising in terraces to a summit crowned by a large crucifix and four flagpoles carrying the national flags of Germany and Italy, and the flags of the European Union and the *Volksbund Deutsche Kriegsgraberfürsorge*, or German War Graves Commission.

Some good views across the Rapido valley and the lower slopes of the mountains can be found from the cemetery grounds, and from here the routes followed by the troops of 34th (US) Division and the French Expeditionary Corps can be seen, when they advanced into the lower stretches of the massif.

Looking north-eastwards across the valley towards the village of Sant' Elia, the path taken by the 3rd Algerian Division in its advance to the west can be seen. The Division captured a line running from Sant' Elia to Valvori by 17 January 1944, having worked its way across the mountains beyond. The French then crossed the Rapido north of Caira and pushed into the Colle Belvedere massif, which rises to the north of

182

the village. A walk to that side of the cemetery gives a worms-eye view of the slopes up which they had to advance. We will look at them from a different perspective later on.

To the south of the cemetery the view is over the road in the valley towards Colle Maiola. 34th (US) Division entered the mountains between here and the Barracks which you passed earlier. 133 RCT swung south on the slopes overlooking the valley and pushed towards the Castle, while 135 Regiment drove on up the valley before you on 1 February, capturing Caira village.

The regiment advanced under cover of fog, and had little difficulty in pushing behind the German defences onto Colle Maiola and Monte Castellone, both of which they occupied by 1000 hours. The fog had considerably helped them achieve surprise. Although their positions on Castellone were the objective of a German counterattack – unsuccessfully – the GIs moved from Maiola southwards towards Snakeshead Ridge. By the end of 2 February, they were within 850 yards of Point 593; two days' later, within 200 yards. From Castellone, a battalion advanced along Phantom Ridge and took Point 706, although their attempt to progress further onto Colle Sant' Angelo was beaten back.

Caira provided the base from which these operations were supported. All of the supplies were taken up into the mountains from here, either up the path seen earlier rising from the Caruso Road north

May 1944: German defences: a Panther turret employed as a pillbox on the Senger Line. Associazone Battaglia di Cassino

of the Barracks, or directly up the valleys which can be seen from the cemetery. Casualties came back down the same routes – a steady stream of them – to the aid posts established in the village buildings. General Ryder, commander of 34th (US) Division, recorded that over 1,000 mules and 700 litter bearers were required over and above the normal transport and medical personnel to cope with the load. The progress of the wounded in the appalling weather conditions, on snow and ice and under fire from the enemy, could only have added to their pain and distress. The intention of the medics was to apply sufficient first aid to allow the casualties to get back as far as possible, as fast as possible, to give them as much a chance of surviving as possible.

After the New Zealand Corps relieved the Americans Caira became the concentration area for 7 Indian Brigade's attempt along Snakeshead Ridge, the story of which was recounted earlier in this book. Caira was not, however, a soft option. Under observation from the heights of Monte Cairo, to the west, artillery shells were a regular hazard to those huddled in the valley below. The Germans recognised the importance of this location to the Allies' activity in the mountains above and paid it appropriate attention from their guns on the surrounding peaks.

From the southern edge of the German Cemetery, looking over the rooftops lining the street below and up the re-entrant to the south, between Colle Maiola and Monte Castellone, can be seen the northern end of Cavendish Road. It starts in this valley and climbs along the western side of the re-entrant, and its path may be made out as a scar

The northern end of the Cavendish Road, which starts from the valley in Caira Village, opposite the German Cemetery. Courtesy the Polish Institute

on the hillside, below the crestline. It was from here that the armoured attack (described earlier) penetrated up to the area of Albaneta Farm.

Following the Third Battle, the Indian Division was withdrawn from the Caira area, to be replaced by 78th ('Battleaxe') Division. The Division came under command of the New Zealand Corps on 17 February 1944, but had played only a peripheral part in the Cassino fighting thus far. The Division comprised 11, 36 and 38 (Irish) Brigades.

78th ('Battleaxe') Division

After a brief spell of only five days on the banks of the Rapido, 38 (Irish) Brigade moved into Caira to relieve French troops on the slopes of Monte Cairo. From their new positions the Ulstermen could look down on the battlefield. It was not to be a relaxing contemplation of the view, however. The 6 Royal Inniskilling Fusiliers held a position which overlooked the Monastery itself, 2 London Irish Rifles were on the commanding heights of Monte Castellone to their north, and 1 Royal Irish Fusiliers held the valley from Caira village westwards towards Monte Cairo. Brigade Headquarters was situated on the edge of the village itself, in a house which had already been damaged by shellfire. The village was accurately registered for artillery fire by the Germans, whose activities soon gave it the title of 'the most heavily shelled pinpoint in Italy'. With excellent observation positions on Monte Cairo it could not have been otherwise, and Brigade Headquarters attracted an undue amount of attention from the German gunners. Daylight movement in most of the Irish positions invited a 'stonk', and everything was carried out under the cover of darkness, including an aggressive patrolling policy by which no-man's land was dominated.

Yet again, it is almost invidious to select one act of heroism from the many that occurred in this area of the battlefield, but that of the Brigade's Roman Catholic Padre is worthy of mention. The citation for his well-deserved Military Cross read:

> *Rev Kelleher was at Battalion HQ in the Caira area when heavy shelling was reported in Caira village causing several casualties to one of the platoons. The Rev Kelleher immediately raced to the village, which was under very heavy shelling. He found the wounded men and assisted the stretcher bearers in their work, carrying wounded in his arms, at great personal risk, to the shelter of a ruined building.*

He comforted the badly wounded men and assisted the overworked stretcher bearers in applying bandages to their wounds.

His cheerfulness and practical assistance undoubtedly saved the

May 1944: Canadian troops advancing in the Liri valley.
Associazone Battaglia di Cassino

His cheerfulness and practical assistance undoubtedly saved
lives of two men and gave fresh proof of his unfailing devotion to d
After handing the sector over to the Poles, the Brigade withdre
Formicola to prepare for its role in Operation DIADEM.

Continue up the hill into the village of Caira, until the sign to Tere
seen on a **small road to the right**. Take this turning and follow the
upwards through a series of bends, **stopping at the fourth left-b
hairpin**. The view across the whole of the Rapido valley is well w
the journey, and an excellent overview of the northern end of the ba

May 1944: a STUG IV destroyed by 78th Division in its advance up the Liri valley. Associazone Battaglia di Cassino

its approaches, and a very clear view of the re-entrant up which Cavendish Road runs can be seen. From left to right may be seen Monte Trocchio, standing proud in the valley, the Rapido, and then the Cassino massif, with the Monastery jutting above the mountains which run towards it from Caira. The commanding position of the German obser-vation points is readily apparent, and you can appreciate the

May 1944: infantry from 8th (Indian) Division occupy the airfield at Aquino.
Associazone Battaglia di Cassino

importance of the positions on the mountainside and the part the French Expeditionary Corps played in clearing them in late January and early February 1944. 3/7 Algerian Tirailleurs attacked up the mountain slopes through the point on which you are standing, on 27 January, and 2/4 Tunisian Tirailleurs advanced just to the north, behind you.

For an interesting series of perspectives on the battlefield, **continue up the mountain towards Terelle village**. Shortly before reaching it, there is a road to your left signposted to Villa S. Lucia which takes you along the slopes of Monte Cairo and onwards to the Liri valley, where you can get stunning views of the locations of the various battles from the heights. For German observers here in 1944, it was possible to follow events as if watching from theatre seats. Once down in the Liri valley, it is but a short drive back into Cassino.

Overlooking the Liri valley, having approached it across the mountains as just described, or directly from Cassino itself by driving down the SS6 (the old Route 6, running close to the foot of the mountains), good views of the advance taken by the Allied armies after the Fourth Battle can be seen from Piedmonte. Drive up into the village to the north of the road until the small loop road around the summit is reached. From here it is possible to look across to Aquina. Post-war development and the growth of vegetation has altered the ground below you, and it is difficult to identify the location of the small villages that were here in 1944. A degree of imagination is necessary to picture the scene as it would have been in May of that year, with German blocking lines at vital locations, and the press of vehicles moving forward. It will be remembered from the campaign description given earlier in this book that the roads at the time were not capable of carrying the amount of traffic that the Allies tried to push along them in their rush towards Rome.

INDEX

General Mark Clark presenting a campaign ribbon to the 100th Infantry Battalion – the Japanese-American Nisei – which fought as part of the 34th (US) Division. The unit served at both Cassino and Anzio.

General Sir Henry Maitland Wilson, who took over the appointment of Supreme Allied Commander Mediterranean in December 1943 when General Eisenhower moved to England to take command of the cross-Channel invasion.

Lieutenant General Wladyslaw Anders, commander of II Polish Corps. The Poles were keen to participate in the battle for Cassino for several reasons, including raising the profile of their country's post-war status. Fearing domination by the Soviets, they needed to bring their situation to the world's headlines.

American troops offloading equipment at Anzio. The limited numbers of Landing Ships Tank in the Mediterranean placed great constraints on Allied planning.

A Bofors antiaircraft gun in the ruins of Cassino after the battle. Although the threat from enemy aircraft was much reduced, it was still necessary to be on guard against hit-and-run raiders.